RESPONDING
AFTER SUICIDE

of related interest

Suicide Prevention Techniques
How a Suicide Crisis Service Saves Lives
Joy Hibbins
ISBN 978 1 78592 549 8
eISBN 978 1 78450 949 1

New Approaches to Preventing Suicide
A Manual for Practitioners
Edited by David Duffy and Tony Ryan
ISBN 978 1 84310 221 2
eISBN 978 1 84642 010 8

A Comprehensive Guide to Suicidal Behaviours
Working with Individuals at Risk and their Families
David Aldridge and Sergio Pérez Barrero
ISBN 978 1 84905 025 8
eISBN 978 0 85700 515 1

Working with Suicidal Individuals
A Guide to Providing Understanding, Assessment and Support
Tony White
ISBN 978 1 84905 115 6
eISBN 978 0 85700 224 2

After the Suicide
Helping the Bereaved to Find a Path from Grief to Recovery
Kari Dyregrov, Einar Plyhn and Gudrun Dieserud
ISBN 978 1 84905 211 5
eISBN 978 0 85700 445 1

Things Jon Didn't Know About
Our Life After My Husband's Suicide
Sue Henderson
ISBN 978 1 78592 400 2
eISBN 978 1 78450 766 4

RESPONDING
AFTER SUICIDE
A PRACTICAL GUIDE TO
IMMEDIATE POSTVENTION

ANDREA WALRAVEN-THISSEN

Foreword by Dr. Sharon McDonnell

Jessica Kingsley *Publishers*
London and Philadelphia

The information on suicide myths featured in the Introduction has been reproduced with kind permission from the World Health Organization.

The information on responsible reporting after suicide featured in the Chapter 4 has been reproduced with kind permission from the World Health Organization.

First published in 2020
by Jessica Kingsley Publishers
73 Collier Street
London N1 9BE, UK
and
400 Market Street, Suite 400
Philadelphia, PA 19106, USA

www.jkp.com

Library of Congress Cataloging in Publication Data
A CIP catalog record for this book is available from the Library of Congress

British Library Cataloguing in Publication Data
A CIP catalogue record for this book is available from the British Library

ISBN 978 1 78592 561 0
eISBN 978 1 78450 958 3

Printed and bound in Great Britain

Contents

Foreword

Losing someone to suicide (personally or professionally) can have a serious effect on an individual's mental health. Many struggle to cope, feel helpless, hopeless, stigmatized, isolated and unsupported, and are also at risk of dying by suicide. Professionals who come into contact with those bereaved by suicide are often anxious and uncertain how to respond.

This issue is especially pertinent to members of the emergency services who come into contact with families bereaved by suicide, at the place of death or when they have to notify the family. It is imperative that we do not underestimate the complexities and difficulties, both emotional and practical, experienced by frontline staff dealing with these issues.

This is a very practical and easy-to-read book, which focuses on the immediate response after suicide, termed postvention. It is written by someone who understands the complexity of suicide and the difficulties faced by first responders and those bereaved by suicide. Andrea shares her wealth of experience of providing immediate suicide postvention to those bereaved by suicide while working alongside emergency services. She provides realistic scenarios which explore some of the difficulties frontline staff might face when they come into contact with those bereaved by suicide, and suggests how specific issues and concerns might be addressed with compassion and sensitivity. This will ultimately help to empower professionals and those bereaved by suicide, which has the potential to save lives.

This book is relevant to those who come into contact with or are responsible for the care of those bereaved by suicide during the early stages of their loss. This includes policy makers, those working in emergency services, funeral directors, clergy, teachers, those responsible for implementing suicide prevention strategies, commissioners who fund services and, equally important, management who need to understand the difficulties their staff face when dealing with responding to and caring for this vulnerable population at a time of high risk and intense need. I highly recommend this book.

Dr. Sharon McDonnell
Managing Director, Suicide Bereavement UK
and Honorary Research Fellow, University of Manchester

Preface

Important information

This book contains very specific and graphic information on what happens after suicide. This was necessary in order to explain to the reader what is important.

If you are recently bereaved or feeling vulnerable, this may not be a suitable book to read at this moment.

The cases in this book have all been adapted to anonymize them; any resemblance to actual cases, names, and locations is coincidental.

The experience in this book was derived while working in different countries. In German-speaking countries, crisis intervention teams are dispatched alongside other emergency services. We don't just respond to suicide but are also sent out to accidental or criminal deaths. It is important to know that we are not clinicians, but first responders; we are trained to work at active police scenes. We set up psychosocial support for civilians and for the first responders working in the incident response. This book is not a guide on how to set up a similar system, but I do hope it will motivate policy makers to consider a similar structure.

Evidence-based suicide postvention training and expertise are available (if you want to learn more, you will find links in the Resources).

Dear reader...

Thank you for taking the time and effort to pick up this book.

It is very strange to write to you. I am about to take you along on some very difficult calls. But I can't see you and walk alongside you while you read. You have to decide on the tempo and the route you will take through the book. Take your time and practice self-care.

Reading and talking about suicide is something we would all rather not do, because it confronts us with our own vulnerabilities and our own lived experience.

The sad reality is that, as first responders, we will all be confronted with suicide. Although I received many different kinds of crisis intervention training, I was not sufficiently prepared to provide suicide postvention efficiently when I first started responding. This book is actually the book I wish I could have had 20 years ago; it answers a very broad spectrum of questions, which I had to answer while learning-by-doing.

When responding after suicide, the primary damage we encounter is irreversible: life is lost. But there is a lot we can do to prevent secondary damage. There are many questions that may be asked. There are many uncertainties and difficulties we face when we are called to respond.

It is so very important to be able to explain to the bereaved what is being done and why this is necessary.

Throughout the book you will hear me talk about ways to help people find action perspectives, to regain control in an extremely difficult situation.

This is actually the core of what we do during crisis intervention work. Action perspectives and experiencing a sense of control are contrary to the feelings we often see after suicide; feelings of despair, helplessness and hopelessness are very common and difficult to handle.

Taking control is a direct antidote to helplessness. You will recognize this in many of the case studies in this book.

I hope to be able to add some information to your knowledge and experience; please take what you need from this book but know that there is no fixed protocol for immediate suicide postvention. Evidence-based training and support are available if you feel you need to learn more in some areas.

My field of work is one of continued education. When I graduated many years ago, I thought I knew it all; I was about to tackle all calls and make every situation better. The reality was quite different; when we are called out to a suicide, all is lost. Working for many, many years has made me humble.

My heart goes out to all the bereaved people who have allowed me to come alongside them on the darkest days of their lives. I know that many of them are hoping that this book will help raise awareness. We need to do better…for them.

I want to thank everyone at Jessica Kingsley Publishers for trusting me to write a book. And for supporting me with a lot of love and patience throughout the process.

A huge thank you to my loved ones and my colleagues, who encouraged me to keep going and get to the result you are now holding. I couldn't have done this without them.

Now, let's get started; there are calls that await you on the pages ahead.

A.W-T.

Introduction

This chapter will give you a basic understanding of what suicide is and what this book is about. You will read about suicide risks, impacts, and myths, and about the importance of words and views. I will explain what suicide postvention is and how it can be used in acute situations, when there are high levels of acute stress, to mitigate feelings of powerlessness.

This book is for all of you confronted with and involved in the immediate aftermath of a suicide. If you are a police officer, you will probably see dozens of suicides during your career. Ambulance staff, fire brigade professionals, doctors, and coroners will also be called after a suicide has occurred. Crisis intervention teams and bereavement services may be available and dispatched. These are just a few professions that suicide affects, but many more professionals will be involved after someone has taken their own life; teachers at school, employers, colleagues, clergy, funeral professionals, GPs (general practitioners), social workers, hospital staff, and prison staff will often be affected and/or involved. This book is for everyone who wants or needs to learn more about what is important during the aftermath of a suicide.

I have responded to many suicides during almost two decades of my professional career. But when I started, I was completely unprepared for what I was about to encounter. In this book I will answer questions I often receive and pass on what I have learned. Much of this I could not find in the literature when I needed it. I feel it should be basic knowledge and become part of basic training, because the sad reality is that every first responder will have to respond to suicide.

The subject of suicide is so complex that I can't offer you quick fixes and simple answers. I hope I can help you find your own solutions and tools to enlarge your personal toolkit. You will read that *you are your own instrument*. That really is the case: read and learn, but adapt the input so that it matches your personal values and expertise. Please use the Resources section at the back of the book or contact me if you need more.

I was born in the Netherlands and currently live in Germany. As a psychiatric nurse, I specialized in psychotraumatology. I later became a first responder and critical incident manager. I lecture and teach in several countries and advise national and European policy makers on psychosocial issues and strategic and tactical emergency management.

I lead Suicide Bereavement UK's (SBUK) crisis support service, offering consultancy and training in suicide postvention. SBUK has developed the first evidence-based suicide postvention training available worldwide. We organize an annual international conference in Manchester and are currently leading the largest scientific survey ever done on the subject of suicide bereavement.

During more than 20 years in the field I have learned to be humble; there is so much we still don't know and need to research. My profession is one that needs continued education and the constant combining of research and experience. Together we can do so much more!

Before we start

If any part of this book triggers suicidal thoughts in you, please take care. Talk to someone or go online to find support that fits your personal needs; in every country many confidential sources of free support are available. Go to the back of the book to find a few suggested links.

It's OK to not be OK, but please remember: suicide does not end the chances of life getting worse—suicide eliminates the possibility of it ever getting better.

This first chapter will give you some general insights into the broad field of suicidology. I have kept it concise on purpose, but you will find reading recommendations in the back of the book, should you want to learn more. There are many good books and links available on the background and science of suicide.

What is suicide?

The word *suicide* is derived from Latin and is often translated as "the deliberate killing of oneself." *Sui-* means "oneself" and *-cide* is derived from *caedere*, which means "to slay" or "to strike." After reading this book, you will understand that both the *deliberate* and the *killing* aspects in the phrase need a different translation.

Much has been written by many on the subject of suicide, and in Chapter 5 you can read about how our views of suicide have changed through the centuries. Writers have attempted to describe the complex subject of suicide from sociological, psychological, epidemiological, historical, and biological points of view. I have studied many of their writings, but the work of suicidologist Edwin Shneidman has been the most important to me. He studied suicide for over 50 years, by studying the literature, but most of all by doing research while directly working with those involved: people who had planned to end their lives but survived.

There is not one definition of suicide that grasps its full complexity. But I will explain that there are certain factors and similarities to be found by studying cases of suicide. And that people who die by suicide don't consciously *choose death*. They *choose to end suffering*.

What this book is not about

Being Dutch, I am very familiar with the many dilemmas surrounding physician-assisted dying. This is a very complex subject on its own, viewed very differently in different countries. I currently live in Germany, where I can't even use the word *euthanasia*, because it is still a very painful word, reminding people of the atrocities of World War II. Physician-assisted dying is not an option in Germany.

In the Netherlands, just an open border away, euthanasia is offered and discussed openly on a daily basis—a huge contrast. I view euthanasia as a subdomain of the broader field of suicidology, and so whenever the subject is discussed, it should be done so respecting suicide-reporting (media) guidelines (see Chapter 4). However, although some of the information in this book may apply, this book is *not* about physician-assisted dying.

This book is also not about another complex field of study; it is not about self-harm, parasuicide, indirect suicide, or subintentional death. These are all terms you will find in the literature, with their own specific definitions and backgrounds. These refer to cases where people hurt themselves or take extreme risks, endangering their lives. There are many different reasons people take such risks, and many different examples to be found: some people injure themselves, some people abuse drugs, others show extreme behavior in traffic, and some play Russian roulette.

Although self-harm behavior increases suicide risk, this book is *not* about self-harm or subintentional death. (There is one exception, a case you will find in Chapter 6.)

Suicide in numbers

The World Health Organization collects data, and if you follow the links given in the back of the book, you will find current lists of suicide rates by country and continent. You can also find many listings of suicide rates using many different markers: by gender, age, ethnicity, profession, religion, etc. What do the numbers mean? You may read "USA 13.9." This means that, in the USA, for every 100,000 people 13.9 will have died by suicide in that year. Numbers in Western countries vary roughly between 8 and 14, but they are "just" numbers. Let's look at an example.

In the USA, the official final suicide rate for the year 2016 was 13.9 people per 100,000 residents. Over 75 percent of those who died by suicide were males. In young people (aged 15–24) suicide is the second-ranking cause of death in the USA. Every 11.7 minutes in 2016 someone died by suicide in the USA.

Let me repeat that: in 2016, *every 11.7 minutes the call needed to be made to send first responders out to a suicide.*

My colleague Julie Cerel is a suicide exposure researcher and former President of the American Association of Suicidology. She has looked into the impact of suicide on those who are left behind—she calls them "suicide loss survivors." Her research-based estimate suggests that every suicide affects 135 people. Of those, more than six experience a major life disruption. Look up the suicide rates in your own country and do the math: *suicide has a major impact on society.*

Worldwide, each day, around 2000 lives will be lost to suicide, directly affecting hundreds of thousands of lives. Many countries are recognizing the severity of the issue and implementing suicide prevention strategies.

How people die

When I studied at a psychiatric hospital, a long time ago, I was taught that women use "soft" methods to end their lives (e.g. take medications) and men use more violent methods (e.g. guns). When training new colleagues, I stay away from generalizing. It may be that the above is the case in your country, but I have seen that the reality doesn't always match.

If you want to know more about specific methods leading to death by suicide in your country, there will probably be statistics you can find online; most countries have (often confidential) sections in death registration forms containing information about causes of death. This data is anonymized and included in national statistics, which can then be used by policy makers. Suicide prevention needs to receive more attention, and these statistics can help us to show politicians how real and devastating suicide is in our society.

So how do people die? A very simple answer is that people choose methods that are easily accessible to them. In the US, where guns are generally readily available, we see many gun suicides (about half of all suicides). Medical professionals often use medications to end their lives; police officers often use their guns. If there is a railway track near a psychiatric hospital, we see more people dying by railway suicide. High-rise buildings or bridges are often used when people jump. Many people refer to certain locations as "hotspots" when multiple suicides occur there. This may help us as professionals to think about prevention at those locations; on bridges you will see fences or signs with messages and even emergency phones connected to helplines. I think we should be reluctant to talk openly about hotspots; people experiencing suicidality may be triggered and directed to those locations, possibly even drawn to them if we point them out.

Some suicides seem to be carried out with a huge amount of aggression, damaging a body severely. But we also see situations where the deceased has tried to prepare a situation to be least harmful to those who will find them afterwards. I use the word "tried" here, because the effect is often very different, as we can never predict the reactions and responses people may experience.

Suicide myths

The World Health Organization has debunked a number of myths about suicide. It's important to share them (you can download them from the link at the back of this book).[1]

Myth: Once someone is suicidal, he or she will always remain suicidal.

Fact: Heightened suicide risk is often short-term and situation-specific. While suicidal thoughts may return, they are not permanent and an individual with previously suicidal thoughts and attempts can go on to live a long life.

Myth: Talking about suicide is a bad idea and can be interpreted as encouragement.

Fact: Given the widespread stigma around suicide, most people contemplating suicide do not know who to speak to. Rather than encouraging suicidal behavior, talking openly can give an individual other options or the time to rethink his/her decision, thereby preventing suicide (more on this in Chapter 4).

Myth: Only people with mental disorders are suicidal.

Fact: Suicidal behavior indicates deep unhappiness but not necessarily mental disorder. Many people living with mental disorders are not affected by suicidal behavior, and not all people who take their own lives have a mental disorder.

Myth: Most suicides happen suddenly without warning.

Fact: The majority of suicides are preceded by warning signs, whether verbal or behavioral. Of course, there are suicides that occur without warning, but it is important to understand warning signs and to look out for them.

Myth: Someone who is suicidal is determined to die.

Fact: On the contrary, suicidal people are often ambivalent about living or dying. Someone may act impulsively. Access to emotional support at the right time can prevent suicide.

---

1   Reprinted from *Preventing suicide: a global imperative – Myths*, The World Health Organization, Copyright 2019. Accessed on 3/11/2019 at www.who.int/mental_health/suicide-prevention/myths.pdf

Myth: People who talk about suicide do not mean to do it.

Fact: People who talk about suicide may be reaching out for help or support. A significant number of people contemplating suicide are experiencing anxiety, depression and hopelessness, and may feel that there is no other option.

Risk factors

What causes suicide? If there was a simple answer, we would be better able to prevent it. Sadly, there is no quick fix. Many studies have been done, and many suicide risk factors have been found, but there is no general answer.

More men than women die by suicide, and past suicide attempts or self-harm increase suicide risk. Limited access to mental healthcare and easy access to lethal methods may be factors. Suffering from mental and/or physical illness can lead to suicidal thoughts and behaviors. Within the LGBTQ community, more people die by suicide compared with the overall population. Socio-economic factors seem to influence suicide risk: poverty and job insecurity may cause people to worry. Divorce is often mentioned, especially when male suicide is discussed. Certain professions seem to increase suicide risk; first responders, doctors, and nurses, but also builders and farmers seem to be at a higher risk. Pressure and stress on the job will have an influence. Being in prison increases suicide risk. And we know that people confronted with a suicide are at a higher risk of dying from suicide themselves.

I always thought the dark winter months would increase suicide risk, but we actually see slightly more suicides during springtime. The increase in sunlight may be a factor, resulting in a slight increase in physical energy. But we really don't know.[2]

Suicide can happen anywhere, anytime, and to anyone.

Several questionnaire models have been developed to help professionals assess suicide risk. But there is no way to assess who will die by suicide and who won't. There is no blood test, no imaging machine, no DNA marker to predict (and thus prevent) suicide.

---

2   See https://blogs.scientificamerican.com/mind-guest-blog/the-persistent-myth-of-holiday-suicide

Is suicide contagious?

We often see multiple suicides within one family, community, or work setting. Bereaved family members have desperately told me they felt as if they were born at risk, having looked at their family history. When mental illness is a factor leading up to the suicide, there may be a hereditary factor in the specific illness. But not everyone suffering from mental illness will die by suicide.

After studying the literature and encountering many cases of multiple suicides, I have come to the conclusion that suicide can be contagious. If someone dies by suicide, this may become seen as an acceptable way to end suffering in certain settings. Others who are suffering themselves may be encouraged to copy what happened.

We often talk about "suicide contagion" when this happens. I recently attended a lecture on this subject by Dr. Alexandra Pitman, a British research psychiatrist. She explained that she would like us to find different wording and used the words "suicide suggestion" to describe this phenomenon. Something to think about and consider:

Words have impact

When I hit puberty, I often got into fights with my mom. During one fight she said I was turning into my dad and she didn't like it. My dad killed himself when I was eight years old. After the fight my mom said she was sorry and didn't mean what she had said, but I kept hearing it, like a little voice in my head. One day I received a very bad grade at school. I was afraid to go home. And I heard that voice in my head, telling me I was just like my dad. I went to the train track where my dad died. Someone saw me and called the police.

This is important to recognize, because in such cases providing *suicide postvention* may actually turn out to be *suicide prevention* as well.

Increased risk

The funeral had passed, and I was just miserable. The first week had been so very busy and I survived it in a dizzy haze. But there I was, all alone. My body was aching, my heart was broken, and I was actually jealous of him; his pain was over. I wanted my pain to be gone too. I went to my medicine drawer and I counted the medication I had in there.

And I scared myself by doing so. I closed the drawer and I called my GP's office. My friend came over and together we threw out any dangerous pills. She took them. It was what I needed that day.

When you read about the guidelines for communicating after suicide (Chapter 4), you will see it is very important not to idealize a suicide after it has occurred. It is important to talk about the person who died and not focus on how and why they died.

You are reading this book because you want to learn more about responding *after* suicide. But if you can, please find some time to take one of the many suicide prevention courses available. I have put a link in the Resources list that will take you to a free UK course. Anyone can learn some basic steps that may save a life; you will learn to *see* signs of possible suicidality. You will learn what to *say*. And you will learn to *signpost* people toward hope and help.

It is common for people who are left behind to experience suicidal thoughts themselves. During suicide postvention we need to address these. When in doubt, just ask the most important question, in a very straightforward way: *Are you considering suicide yourself?*

Postvention = prevention
Constriction
Professor Edwin Shneidman was a pioneer in the field of suicidology. He studied suicide for many decades and left us many excellent books to learn from. He wrote about a phenomenon he called *constriction*. The term is derived from Latin and actually means "to become narrow under pressure." When people are suicidal, their worldview narrows. They experience extreme suffering and something similar to tunnel vision; they see death only as a way to end suffering. The suffering takes up so much energy that they are really not able to make conscious decisions, weighing all the consequences; they just need to find a way to end what they are experiencing. *Suicide is a way to end the pain, it's not a conscious decision to choose death.*

Psycheache
Another Shneidman term I want to mention is *psycheache*, pointing to intolerable emotions, unbearable pain, and unacceptable anguish. I don't have a good translation into my other languages for the word, so

I only use it in English, but the word itself really got to me when I first read about it. Psycheache causes people to experience life as intolerable. It may overwhelm us temporarily. If you have ever experienced psycheache, you will understand what I mean.

When people are suicidal and experience psycheache, their suffering absorbs their thinking. Again: *Death may become a solution to end this pain. It is not a conscious decision to choose death.*

If you have ever informed people that their loved one died by suicide, you may have seen psycheache up close and personal. Your message may lead to tremendous feelings of hopelessness and powerlessness. We can't bring back the person who died. But we can work with those who are left behind and help them mitigate these feelings. We can't change what happened, but we can be there for them, with them. Walk alongside them when every direction may seem to be lost. *"I am here for you. You are not alone."*

That's what suicide postvention is all about. A suicide takes away any hope of a future and ways to make things better. People become vulnerable and sometimes even suicidal themselves. This is why we feel that postvention is also prevention.

Your views

Before we start, I would like to ask you to perform a little self-reflection task. You are reading a book on suicide, but how do you view this difficult subject? Start with the way you talk about suicide. Be specific: which words do you use when you talk about it?

When training (first) responders or responding to a suicide myself, I always listen very closely to the words people use, because they matter. Some people will speak about "self-murder," which holds a certain negative attitude if you look at the meaning behind the words. You may say, "He *committed* suicide," which adds weight to the act itself. Many people will say, "He killed himself." Which words do you use? Are they neutral? How do you view suicide?

I am a native Dutch and German speaker, and in both of these languages *suicide* can be used as both verb and noun. This is a very direct and neutral way to talk about suicide.

There is no right or wrong here, but when we go out to suicide calls, it is important to be aware of the impact words may have.

Listening

I arrived at the brother's house and asked him if he would tell me what had happened. When telling me, he said a few times that his brother went out and murdered himself. There was a strong conviction within these words. I took notice. Later we spoke about it and it turned out there was a strong religious view on suicide within this family. There was a huge amount of anger and aggression hidden behind this brother's choice of words.

This brother had very strong thoughts and feelings, very different from my own. But I was able to support him by listening and reflecting.

You may have strong views on suicide yourself, and that is OK. If you work in a religious setting, you may even actively use them. As first responders, however, we should always stay neutral; we support anyone, anytime, anywhere, without judgment or prejudice. Easier said than done, but very important!

Back to you… Which words do you use when you talk about suicide? Are you a native English speaker or do you think in a different language? Are your words neutral? Or are there other words available in your language? In the English language there are several options to choose. Bereaved people have told us they would like to see following choice of wording:

- "He ended/took his own life."

- "He died by suicide."

Nothing more, nothing less; and it is not complicated.

Bereaved people also told us how important it is that we use their loved one's name when talking about them. As first responders, we tend to talk in tactics or technics, about "bodies" and "cases." I get it, because it can also help to put some distance between us and "the case"; responding to suicide is demanding, and we often identify with certain aspects within a case. But it is important to talk about the *person* who died.

Detail

The policeman was talking about the DNA material they would need to identify Jonathan. I noticed the mother kept answering and using a different name. I asked her what she called her son. She explained that everyone called him Nat, because he really disliked being called Jonathan. We offered to speak about Nat instead.

Good listening, a simple question, and a small change, but this mother later told me how important it had been to her.

The examples of adapting wording are ways to work towards what I call "psychological alignment." My definition of psychological alignment is quite simple: we find people where *they* are. This is always different from where *I* am. It's a mindset which requires empathy.

After a suicide everyone will react differently, because every person is unique and has a unique past and a unique set of coping skills. Expect to encounter every and any reaction on a very broad scale: people may become frantic, panic, completely lose control, or they may go completely numb, and some may not visibly react at all. I have seen all these extremes, and many reactions in-between, but it is very important that we work with what we see.

Imagine a high-rise building. The person you are going to support is on a different reaction level of the building. To be able to find the person, I will get into a virtual elevator. And I will find ways to join the person on their level. This is not always easy, but I hope this book will give you some tools to help you find and support people in different ways. To find them where *they* are.

In Chapter 5 you will read more about boundaries, because we are walking a delicate line; it is important our presence is real and empathetic. But when empathy becomes sympathy, we are crossing a line. Always make sure your elevator is waiting to take you back to your own floor.

What is suicide postvention?

You have probably used the words "prevention" and "intervention" before, maybe even in relation to suicide. In Latin, the verb *venire* means "to arrive," *pre* means "before," *inter* means "between" and *post* means "after." So *suicide postvention* literally means "arriving after suicide." Suicide prevention aims to reduce risk factors and increase protective factors and resilience. Intervention means we engage with people before suicidal thoughts lead to suicidal behavior, offering care and support. In suicide postvention, we assist those bereaved by suicide. They are at risk of suicide themselves, which is why we say that suicide postvention is prevention. In this book we focus on immediate postvention.

Take a moment to think about your own country. If a suicide is reported, who will be part of the response? Who will be called to the first response and who will follow up? In my view, all of the people and services involved are suicide postventionists.

Very well, but when a sudden death is called in, it is technically and officially not a suicide yet, because an investigation, and in some countries an inquest, is needed before we can call it a suicide.

Good point and I'm glad you made it.

Everything you will read in this book belongs to a broader profession and my field of work. I manage *critical incidents*. Critical incidents are unusually challenging events. They have the potential to create significant human distress by overwhelming usual coping mechanisms in both civilians and/or first responders.

In German-speaking countries, there is 24/7 availability of specialist teams, trained and experienced to respond to critical incidents. Our German system is called PSNV.[3] Most team members respond a few days a month and have day jobs in the army, first response services, social services, pastoral settings, or other helping professions. They have received extensive training and team supervision, because responding to critical incidents is demanding. The teams are dispatched to these unusually challenging events and arrive along with other emergency services.

Calls can come in after fatal traffic incidents, the sudden death of a child, natural or manmade disasters, but there is not really a fixed list of indications—whenever a dispatcher or a first responder in charge feels we are needed, we can be called. Sadly, about half of our calls turn out to be suicides. Sometimes this is expected and mentioned; sometimes we will just respond to the sudden death, not knowing if it was an accident, a suicide, or a violent death.

In this book I will focus on suicide (with one exception in Chapter 6). But the knowledge and interventions we implement and apply during suicide postvention can be used after any critical incident. So, even if the examples and tools I will give you focus on suicide, they may

---

3   Psychosoziale Notfallversorgung (Psychosocial Emergency Service), a uniformed service.

assist you if the sudden death turns out to be a natural, accidental, or violent death.

I have been trained by some amazing colleagues who have passed on their wisdom and experience after many years of service in the field of military psychology and psychiatry. When our teams go out, they implement principles of *crisis intervention* and the science of *psychotraumatology.* The latter field of science is relatively new. Although psychological trauma as we know it has always been around, it was not seriously acknowledged before the two World Wars, when soldiers suffered serious mental illness. Several labels have been invented for their symptoms throughout several wars in history: *soldier's heart* and *shell shock* among them.

After the Vietnam War, psychologists and psychiatrists studied and treated many soldiers, because they came home with severe mental injuries. In 1980 PTSD (post-traumatic stress disorder) was added to the DSM (*Diagnostic and Statistical Manual of Mental Disorders*). For the first time "trauma" could be officially understood and diagnosed as caused by an outside stressor (a critical incident).

The human brain and mind are the focus of much research, and science keeps teaching us more about how they function. But since the field of psychotraumatology is still very young, there is still a lot we don't know!

Back to the Latin: *crisis intervention* means "intervene, to arrive amid crisis." A critical incident has occurred and people are in crisis. It is important to note that we don't look at the incident (the suicide) as being the crisis; crisis is what happens afterwards. Coping mechanisms are overwhelmed and a crisis develops. Because everyone is different, each crisis will be different; a suicide will lead to crisis in the bereaved mother, but it may also cause a crisis in one of the first responders attending. And there may be crises within family or colleague relationships following the suicide.

Crisis intervention—attending to people in crisis—is all about offering a supportive presence. In pastoral care settings, we call this a *ministry of presence.* We can't change what happened and we are not offering therapy. We don't take over; we walk alongside people.

It took me a long time to get this. When I qualified as a psychiatric nurse, I went out to save people, I wanted to change the world. In the past 20 years I have learned to be humble. When I am called to a suicide, all is lost; life and any hope of a better future for the deceased are gone.

This is what makes responding after suicide so very demanding to first responders. We have chosen to become a doctor, nurse, police officer, or fire fighter because we want to help save people. That's what we do best. But we can't after suicide; life is lost.

Suicide doesn't discriminate; it takes lives in every social setting, every profession, every sex and ethnicity; it can happen anytime, anywhere. This causes feelings of powerlessness and hopelessness, and often a huge amount of identification with aspects within a case.

If you speak to people diagnosed with PTSD, they will tell you that they experienced severe feelings of helplessness and hopelessness during the event that led up to their illness. I have discovered that there is an antidote to helplessness. Imagine old-fashioned scales. If you visualize helplessness on the one side, there is a counterweight that can be put on the other side of the scales. It is control. Autonomy.

If people can find ways to take control, their feelings of helplessness diminish. The two are direct counterweights: if one increases, the other goes down (and the other way around). *Everything we do and say during suicide postvention is aimed at mitigating feelings of helplessness and toward regaining control.*

The deceased went alone, and any and every form of control was taken from those who are left behind. Following the suicide, even more control is taken from them: a private room may become a police scene; the body of a loved one is being taken by the state; investigative and very personal questions need to be answered. Privacy is being invaded.

The primary damage (the loss of life) can't be reversed. But we can prevent secondary damage by structuring our response, implementing what science and experience have taught us.

My approach to suicide postvention is about action perspectives. I am to increase a sense of control in those who are left behind—and in all of you who respond to such critical incidents.

For most people, a supportive presence will suffice, but please be aware that on rare occasions immediate referral to specialist care may be necessary. In 20 years I have only seen a few of those cases, but they all had life-threatening implications. *When in doubt, don't hesitate to ask for advice and help!*

We are called to people we don't know. We don't know anything about their medical history. The news of the suicide may cause extreme stress levels to influence physical functioning. This may lead to complications in existing conditions or to new symptoms of illness. If someone experiences sudden severe pain in the chest, it may well be a reaction to stress, but it is something a medical professional should evaluate.

Cindy, 57, who lost her son to suicide

I don't remember everything, but I know I was in the kitchen when it happened. The officers had come to our house and broke the news. When I heard my son was dead, I felt an immediate pain in my chest, as if someone had put a fist in there and was turning it around. I had trouble breathing and an officer had to hold me up. We sat down on the couch, but I really couldn't. I remember they were talking, my husband was talking, but I didn't understand what was said. I just had to get up, I wanted to run, but my legs were wobbly. I stumbled into the kitchen and leaned against the cooker. I felt I couldn't breathe; I vomited and passed out. Thankfully, the officers called an ambulance and I was taken to the cardiac ward of the hospital. The lines on the heart monitor were abnormal, and at first the doctor thought I was having a heart attack. I was later told I had probably experienced Takotsubo cardiomyopathy, also called broken heart syndrome. I had never heard of it and it seems to be very rare. My heart recovered. But it feels like a part of it was lost that day.

When in doubt, don't hesitate to ask for advice and help!

On other very rare occasions, the acute stress may cause immediate serious mental instability, posing a danger to the person's own life or the lives of others. People may become suicidal, and in some cases hospitalization may be necessary.

Peter, 48, who lost his daughter to suicide

I found her. She was gone. My wife came in behind me. She ran to her, she touched her, looking for a heartbeat or a breath, she did everything you are supposed to do. She was shouting at me, but I could not respond. She made the phone call and I just stood there. I froze, my brain froze. I needed to be with my little girl. We had had an argument the day before; I needed to find her, I needed to tell her I was wrong. I needed her back. I can't really explain what happened, but I felt my mind was taken over by this strange urge. Looking back, I am so grateful to the paramedic following me out on to the balcony. Because I was about to jump. After 24 hours in the hospital I woke up and I remembered what had happened. It was as if I was telling the nurse someone else's story, I saw myself, but I really felt that wasn't me. I felt ashamed and embarrassed, I was overwhelmed by guilt, because I had put my wife through so much extra pain. She and I are now both seeing a therapist. There is so much we need to work through. I never wanted to die, but I almost did that day, when we had already lost the most beautiful person that ever walked the earth.

When in doubt, don't hesitate to ask for advice and help!

Suicide and mental illness

A suicide is a disaster and it may lead to the development of serious mental illness in those affected. But it is important to state that this is not the case for the majority of people; they will recover in time and not develop psychopathology (mental illness).

Nowadays serious illness has become part of our daily lingo:

- "I am feeling a bit depressed today…"

- "We were all in shock when we heard…"

- "Oh, look at the poor girl, she looks so traumatized…"

Oh, come on, you know we are just talking about feelings when we use those words, as you can understand from the context. Well, I would like to ask you to stop using them in this context. I will explain to you what happens in the body and the mind when people experience acute stress: it makes them vulnerable. Throwing in big words like *trauma, depression,* or *shock* leads to over-pathologizing; people may be extremely upset, distressed, disturbed, overwhelmed, and emotional after a suicide, but these reactions are healthy reactions we can expect. They can be explained and managed and are *natural* reactions people experience as a response to an *extreme* situation.

In some cultures, emotional reactions are actually encouraged and shared, but in our Western world they have become more and more uncomfortable to us. We are disturbed when people lament, maybe even scream or drop to their knees when we have just told them their loved one has died. We tend to offer them medication to calm down, but who are we actually helping?

In some cases, medication may be needed, but in my experience it is given way too often. Numbing feelings may complicate recovery, experts tell us. Medicating people makes our work easier, but is it always necessary?

I hope this book will offer you alternatives, helping you to support those who are left behind in different ways. If we help people by showing them ways to help themselves and regain control, we are working with their own resilience.

When more is needed

This book is written for those of us working during the immediate aftermath of a suicide. It is important we are aware of bereavement support systems in our regions, states, and countries. Take some time to check out the websites on the materials you may have handed out before. Ask around and inform yourself about what's out there. Do you know how support systems in your area work?

Some people will want to be left alone, but many others will be grateful for information and links to further support. Sometimes we can directly connect them to organizations, and in other cases we leave them the information they need to find help. Every person is different, so advice will be different every time; it is important that we respect and look at personal values, and religious and cultural aspects and wishes. While responding after suicide as crisis interventionists, we carry many flyers and brochures in our backpacks, but we only leave a few of them, and we make sure they fit the needs we see.

Some people will develop serious mental illness after a suicide. There are so many complicating factors surrounding what happened; sometimes grieving becomes so complicated that a grief disorder may be diagnosed. Or depression will set in, making treatment necessary. Previously existing mental illness may return; addiction may become an issue. Or the circumstances surrounding the suicide may lead to post-traumatic stress disorder.

These are just a few examples of complications we see after suicide. As first responders or bereavement supporters, we will not be the ones assessing and diagnosing these complications. I will therefore not list symptoms and criteria. Too often people self-diagnose or stick labels onto others.

We live in a society where diagnostic criteria are needed to convince insurance companies, because professional help is expensive. On the other hand, if you can't return to work just days after your child has died by suicide, you will need to request sick leave, when, really, there is no illness, only tremendous distress. Technically, a person does not qualify to receive a medical diagnosis (yet), but society is arranged in such a way that you are either healthy (joining the workforce) or sick (if you are still upset and not ready to go back to work).

On rare occasions, I encounter employers who get it: they offer employees extended leave after a suicide, or they facilitate other ways of support. I salute them!

Sally, 38, who lost her husband to suicide

When Jim died, our children were 2 and 4 years old. We were both employed by the same employer. The hospital's staff manager called on the fourth day and asked if he could come by for a short visit. I assumed he wanted to bring condolences, but instead he brought a huge notebook. Many, many colleagues had signed or written a few comforting lines, some had written a whole page, all within those few days!

I told him I did not know how and when I would be able to return to work, but then he gave me an even bigger gift: many colleagues at the hospital had offered a few hours of their own leave to me. The hours added up to six weeks of full-time paid leave. I was allowed to take it up as I needed it.

This has been such a huge blessing to me. The time to be with my children and sort everything I needed to arrange was precious, but knowing so many people cared about me was the biggest blessing.

Sally actually went back to work early. There is no right or wrong, no fixed back-to-work-chart. She went to work for one day in the second week, two days in the third, three days in the week after and then back to full-time, while Jim's parents stayed with the children. She never called in sick, but she did see a therapist, who helped her work through complicated grief issues, during the first year after the suicide.

The hospital also offered suicide postvention to their staff and a peer support system was introduced. Two years after Jim's death, Sally joined the peer support team and she is currently implementing hospital suicide prevention strategies.

Words matter

It is important to state that we speak about *reactions* after a suicide. If we speak about *symptoms*, we are talking about illness. And *illness* means there is dysfunction and *treatment* is needed.

When in doubt, please make sure you involve the GP and let them follow up. Make sure you always respect privacy and informed consent; don't take over but facilitate the bereaved in this process.

Next, I will explain what causes the reactions we experience after a suicide. It is important we understand this, so we can explain what we see. Some people call this explanation *psychoeducation*. It really doesn't matter what you call it, but it's important. Let me explain this with an analogy:

> Imagine you catch an influenza virus (the flu) for the first time in your life. You have never heard of it, but suddenly you notice your nose is blocked. You get a sore throat, a cough, and a huge headache. Your fever rises, and since you don't know what is happening, you panic; you feel miserable, your body aches, and you can hardly move. Can this kill you?
>
> You then get a visit from your GP. He takes a deep breath and says you are the fifth flu patient that day. He explains you have caught a nasty virus. Everything you are experiencing is to be expected and he tells you that you will probably feel miserable for a few more days. He gives you advice, tells you to stay in bed, drink plenty of tea, and eat chicken soup. He also wants you to keep an eye on the fever and tells you that on rare occasions people develop complications. He tells you how to recognize them and wants you to call immediately should they occur. But he explains that will probably not be necessary and you will feel better in a few days, because your body is well equipped to fight the flu.

American colleagues will be familiar with this analogy, as it is often told during training. Because everyone gets it when we explain it this way.

Critical incident stress messes with our body and mind. This can be very scary if you don't know what is happening. Explaining won't make the reactions go away, but it will help people to deal with them differently.

Acute stress and how it affects us

During evolution, our brain got bigger and bigger. Our superbrain lets us invent the most amazing things; it allows us to love and feel, and it assists us if we have to make complex decisions. But when we are in danger, we really don't need all these sophisticated functions. During evolution, our *survival mode* was preserved. It's what we call the *fight–flight–freeze response.*

The center of your brain houses your limbic system, also called the emotional brain. When we experience immediate danger, it is activated, like a fire alarm. The brain orders our adrenal glands to produce a huge amount of adrenaline, and our body and mind go into survival mode. Our blood pressure rises, and large muscle groups receive increased blood flow.

Adrenaline

I remember the first time I had to provide CPR in a real situation. I had learned it at nursing school and got so very tired while practicing on Annie the doll. And there I was, confronted with the real deal. I was on my own. I kept going until the first ambulance came. I did not get tired at all. I could have continued much longer! (The patient survived.)

The adrenaline gave me the energy to save a life. I experienced *critical incident stress.* Our body will first produce very high levels of adrenaline, but this puts a huge strain on us. Therefore, cortisol is also produced. It will take a while for our cortisol levels to get up, but they will stay up when the adrenaline levels go down. Our stress system was caught by surprise, so it will keep up the cortisol levels, just in case another emergency follows.

Both adrenaline and cortisol have a huge effect on our body and our mind. Physically, we will be able to run extremely fast, lift heavy weights, or act in other lifesaving ways. But acute stress also changes brain functioning: blood flow increases within the limbic (emotional) system, but more sophisticated (outer) parts of our brain will become less active. This makes sense, because it allows us to respond more quickly to threats when we are in danger. But it can also complicate things.

Speech

We all know the phrase "lost for words." After acute stress, this can be a very real experience. It can be explained if you understand the effect acute (critical incident) stress can have on the brain. The Broca area, also called the *speech center*, is situated in the front left side of our brain. After a suicide, you may encounter people who just can't say a word. Or you may ask them for a certain phone number or address and they just won't be able to tell you.

Often people will say they feel as if they are going crazy, but they are not; their brain is reacting to the extreme stress levels in the body and it may well be that their Broca area has gone offline.

Memory

Imagine a normal day, maybe even today. You are quite relaxed, reading this book, and your senses are taking in information; you see, hear, smell, taste, and touch, and your brain brings everything together, creating an image, a mental picture of a situation. This image is marked with a virtual "time and place" stamp. Tonight you will go to sleep and enter your deep-sleep phase. Your brain will take all the images of today and sort them into your virtual memory folders. Our superbrains are more sophisticated than any library, but imagine old-fashioned filing folders, marked and organized, and putting paperwork into the right folder.

Now back to our critical incident stress. The alarm went off and it is taking up a lot of energy. Our senses are bringing in scary information and horrific images. Because of the changes in brain functioning as a response to the stress hormones, the marking part of our brain (the hippocampus) may tend to go offline; images are not (or not sufficiently) stamped with a "time and place" mark. Fast-forward to the evening. You will fall asleep, but when you enter your deep-sleep phase, there will be a syntax error warning. You may wake up and one of the day's startling images may be all too real for you. What happened? Your superbrain library wanted to start filing the day's images. But the images were not marked, so there was no way to put them into memory folders, because where would they need to go?

Usually, during the days and weeks following critical incident stress, hormone levels and arousal will go down. And people will be able to sort through the images, look at them once again, but this time their brain will add the "time and place" mark. The images will remain just as horrible and awful, but when they are marked, they can become a memory.

This is what happens when we speak about what happened in a setting that feels safe to us. This may be a private setting or a conversation with a bereavement supporter, or maybe even a group. As long as adrenaline levels don't shoot up, we can work through what happened. People trained to support others know when and how to assist people to work through these difficult steps. Training and experience are important, because *well meant* is not automatically *well done*. We don't want to re-traumatize people or experience vicarious (secondary) traumatization ourselves.

It is important to take time to work through the many images—to talk about what happened, although other activities may help as well. Writing about what happened or putting images into art or music can be of huge benefit. Listening to others, sharing similar experiences, can also help to sort out our own images.

Trauma

Sometimes it is not possible to sort and mark images, and they will continue to flare up, maybe even return as flashbacks. They may become so real that people actually relive and re-experience the whole situation. This is what happens when people are traumatized.

There are several ways a therapist can sort out the images and pick out those causing the problems. During therapy it is possible to work through them, marking them on the way, until the mark is so clear that the superbrain can recognize and sort it out, processing the image, so it becomes a stored memory.

Again, we may signpost people toward professional help. But when we offer immediate suicide postvention, we are supporters. We are first responders. If we feel an assessment or a diagnosis and professional care might be needed, we refer people. This is especially important to keep in mind within our teams; some team members may have day jobs offering therapy or mental healthcare. As soon as they put on their crisis intervention uniform, their mindset needs to change. This takes a lot of training and supervision. And not everyone will eventually become a full team member. Sometimes during training and learning, a new member and/or a team will discover that it may be better to part ways. Our work is beautiful and important, but it is demanding and very tough at times.

INTRODUCTION—SUMMARY

- Although suicide literally means the deliberate ending of one's life, we know that most people who die by suicide suffer from serious mental illness. They experience constriction, an altered mental state that leads to a narrowed worldview.

- If all hope is lost, suicide becomes a way to end the pain and suffering they experience. It is not a conscious decision to choose death.
- Suicide takes thousands of lives on a daily basis; anyone, anywhere, can be confronted with suicide.
- The words we choose when talking about suicide can increase or lower suicide risk.
- It is important to know and debunk suicide myths to lower risks and decrease stigma.
- Suicide postvention is the support we give to civilians and first responders after a suicide has occurred.
- This book is about immediate suicide postvention, offered within the first hours after suicide.
- More men than women die by suicide.
- Many risk-increasing factors have been determined, but there is no reliable tool to assess who will die by suicide and who won't.
- Suicide can be contagious.
- People bereaved by or confronted with suicide are at a higher risk of dying by suicide themselves.
- One suicide directly impacts an average of 135 people.
- Many of them will experience severe reactions after a suicide, caused by an acute stress response. It is important we explain this to them.
- They are not ill. They are normal people experiencing normal reactions to an extreme incident.
- Most people will recover without professional help. Postvention, peer support in self-help groups, and bereavement support can be very important in this process.
- Some people may develop physical or mental illness. They will need to be referred to professional healthcare providers.

1

Responding to Suicide

This chapter will explain what needs to be done and what to expect after a sudden death, possibly a suicide, is reported. You will read about police scene and incident management, and about possible reactions you may encounter while responding. Several case studies of immediate suicide postvention will be presented.

Every situation you encounter will be different from any situation I encountered. I will write about situations such as we often see. Read about them with your own perspective in mind.

Sudden death and suicide: Legal protocols

In England and Wales there will be a coroner's investigation and inquest if a death was violent or unnatural, or if the cause of death is unknown. There is a very specific framework of law, passed by Parliament. A coroner can be a legal professional or a doctor appointed by a local authority (council) to an independent judicial office.

The deceased's body will be examined before being released to the bereaved. This may take time, which needs to be explained to people. If time is of the essence, sometimes religious washing rituals or other rituals need to be postponed. The coroner will contact the bereaved to explain what is being done and why this is needed.

Simply put, the coroner will investigate and establish who has died and how, and when and where they died. In other countries, the same questions will be answered, but by medical doctors and within a police investigation. If necessary, people may be asked to view and identify the deceased.

In England and Wales, all the findings of the investigation will be presented in a public hearing in the coroner's court. The bereaved may choose to attend. Sometimes they will be asked to testify. If this is too hard, a written testimony will often suffice.

The hearing is called an inquest. Typically, it is held weeks, months, or sometimes years after the death. The investigation findings will be presented in court and the cause of death (e.g. suicide) will be determined. It will usually be held without a jury in court. Exceptions are cases where people have died in detention, in immigration centers, or if they died while detained under the Mental Health Act. In these cases, a jury will be present.

If the deceased was a well-known person or a celebrity, journalists may attend the inquest. This can be very upsetting to the bereaved. There are services offered to prepare the bereaved beforehand and to support them during the inquest. If you work in the UK, or if you are interested in learning more about the coroner's system, download the brochure included in the Resources list. This brochure will be handed in print to the bereaved. It is important to know the content if you will be supporting them.

Yvonne, 63, who lost her husband to suicide

I am glad I was prepared for the inquest and I knew what would happen. Because many details were shared about Frank's death. Photographs and even a piece of rope he used were shown. It was really strange for me to know that all of this information would become public information. Someone from my bereavement support group went to court with me. The whole inquest lasted for about 40 minutes. It was eerie to realize that Frank was just one of many, when to me he was the world. There was no real emotion, just facts and the verdict; Frank had died by suicide. That was it. I received the death certificate and many of the people in court won't even remember his name. It was a sobering experience. But I am glad it is over now; I had to wait weeks until the inquest. It was something very difficult that was awaiting me.

Wendy, emergency dispatcher

I was on the phone, answering the emergency call from a desperate mother. Her son had left the house, and when she went into his room, she found a farewell note. She was very upset, so it took me a while to be able to ask her for the information I needed. Information on the car he took, on what he was wearing, and so on. I was just about to give her some information about how to proceed when the colleague next to me tapped my shoulder. She shook her head. She had just received another call; a young man had jumped from the roof of an apartment building.

This may look like a very straightforward situation, but it really isn't. Every suicide in every country needs to be investigated by law enforcement and medical professionals. First, a doctor on the scene will conclude that the death did not occur from natural causes. The location where a body is found will be considered a police scene (incident scene) When a suicide is reported, it is actually not yet officially a suicide, so a *sudden death* is called in. An investigation will follow. And this (or a subsequent inquest) may conclude that the death was a suicide.

When a person has gone missing, people are in urgent need of information; especially when safety is of concern, people may be desperate. In this social media world, news travels fast and cannot possibly be contained. On the other hand, it is essential to check facts and information, so as first responders we only share what is validated and verified. Sometimes things seem to be straightforward and we may be tempted to share information quickly, but the investigation may show a different outcome.

Wendy continued

In the dispatch room we were combining both calls, comparing information the callers gave us. But we did not have verified information yet. I did not want the mother to receive potentially devastating news through social media or go out and follow the blue lights rushing through her town towards the apartment building. So I asked her to stay at home and told her I had just sent a patrol car out to her house. The officers would take the missing persons information and stay with her until there was more information.

A death may be from natural causes, it may turn out to be accidental, deliberately or negligently caused by others (homicide), caused by suicide, or a cause of death may not be able to be determined.

Protocols differ in different countries, but in every country, death will be confirmed by a medical professional. This may be clear, but on some occasions lifesaving efforts (e.g. CPR) may have been attempted and will now have to be stopped.

Peter, police officer

We arrived at the apartment building within minutes and we were the first ones responding to the scene. As police officers, we are not medical professionals, but we are trained in first aid. A man and a woman were providing CPR to the young man on the ground. Things did not look good and he was not responding in any way. Since the ambulance was still minutes away, we took over CPR. When our ambulance colleagues arrived, they installed their devices and monitors. There was no sign of life, no way to save it. The young man was pronounced dead, and we took charge of the scene.

The location may suddenly become a police scene, which is clear to us as first responders, but it is important to explain to people what will happen: the body can no longer be touched, and evidence and items will have to be left until those in charge (the police) officially clear the scene. In the case of a (suspected) suicide, an investigation by law enforcement personnel will follow to establish the circumstances surrounding the death.

Sarah, 38, who lost her son to suicide

I found my son in his bedroom. I screamed for his sister, I put him on the floor and started CPR. His sister made the call and I kept going. I had brought back people before, working at the hospital. I was determined to bring my son back to life; this could not be, he was 14 years old; 14-year-old boys just can't die. I was working in an adrenaline haze; I don't remember anything else. Then strong arms picked me up. The ambulance staff. I screamed and shouted at them; they needed to save my boy. But they didn't. They soon said that he had died, but that could not be. I wanted them to let me continue; I would bring him back. I was screaming, kicking, fighting, and they took me away. Looking back, I feel awful. For hurting people who came to help. For not attending to my daughter, who was completely on her own. But it took me a while to get to where I am now. When it happened, I was caught in a frantic haze, in disbelief, like a lioness protecting her young.

To switch from working in rescue mode to working at an incident scene may be especially hard when attempted lifesaving measures were started by people close to the deceased. Performing CPR is a very physical act, and adrenaline levels (already increased after being confronted with the situation) will rise even higher. People will experience a surge of energy and physical strength to keep going. It puts them in an action perspective. If you need to break these efforts, you may potentially encounter aggression, as in Sarah's case:

Sarah continued—crisis intervention

We were called to Sarah's house. Her son had died. We didn't receive much information, just that the emergency call had been made by a young child. And that the mother was aggressive towards first responders. When we arrived, ambulance staff and two police officers were restraining Sarah. She was very vocal and aggressive, kicking the colleagues holding her. In the corner stood a little girl, shaking and pale. My team partner that day was a retired soldier. We looked at each other and without words we divided tasks. He went to support Sarah. She lived in a very rural area and we had seen nobody outside when we arrived. So my colleague took control and announced that he and Sarah would go for a walk. He did not offer her any other option and a police officer went along with them. While walking in the fresh air, my colleague acknowledged Sarah's frustration and he allowed her to voice it. After a while he could explain to Sarah how the adrenaline was affecting her. Being a nurse, she understood this. My colleague also acknowledged her tremendous effort of performing CPR on her own, for over ten minutes; she did an amazing job, but her son had died.

He actively used breathing techniques to help Sarah regain control. After a while, he asked her about the little girl he had seen when we arrived. He advised her on possible ways to support Hannah, and he informed her about the steps and procedures that would need to be taken. Before coming back in, the police officer spoke to Sarah.

I had been tending to 8-year-old Hannah. We found her room and created a safe place for her and made her a little tent under the duvet. She told me what had happened, and I praised the excellent way she had called the emergency number. She was very worried about her mommy, and I told her my colleague was creating a safe place for her, too. I explained that a doctor and some other people were in her brother's room. Hannah started to cry. My comfort bear (a bear wearing the same uniform we wear) appeared. I told her he needed be cuddled and would stay back to support her. In my backpack I had several books, but Hannah had her own books in her room. So we read a book together.

When Sarah's agitation had subsided, my colleague brought her in to be with Hannah. Sarah joined Hannah under the duvet and they cried together. We gave them some privacy.

Meanwhile, the investigation was being done. Questions were answered, information was given, and we stayed to structure the process, guided by the police officer in charge. This was a sad call for everyone involved and I arranged peer support for the first responders.

Hannah showed me pictures of her brother and we did some drawing together, while my colleague supported her mommy. Before the body was taken, the investigators allowed Sarah and Hannah a goodbye. The body was wrapped in a sheet and put on the boy's bed. In this case, we were asked not to touch the body so as to preserve any evidence.

To the police officers, it was important to keep a professional distance; one of them had 14-year-old son, he later told me. When speaking to them, we spoke about "the body" and "the deceased." When speaking to Hannah and Sarah, we made sure the boy's name was used.

I took some candles from my backpack and lit them. Sarah and Hannah then went back into the room where they had found such a horrific scene. They walked into a different scene now. A tremendously sad and heartbreaking scene, but not a horrific one.

After the body was taken, we all sat down in the living room. The ambulance staff and the two police officers who had arrived first returned to the house. In this case, no serious injury was suffered by them and no charges were filed against Sarah. It was important to sit down together and to end a horrifying day.

The first responders went home after an apologetic hug from Sarah. And we left her with her best friend, who had come over. Her GP would come over later and her local bereavement support liaison would follow up the next day.

Why investigate?

The simple answer is because rules and regulations say so. And many people will accept that as an answer. They often need more to understand things better. You are not obliged to explain, but I feel it is a matter of respect to see if you can assist by answering and explaining. Who is responding? What are they doing and why is this necessary?

If respect isn't a sufficient argument, please know that taking a little time to give information can save you a lot of time later—irritations and complaints often arise when people don't feel heard and seen. The human gesture of respecting those we support is enough for me.

Employers and managers often want us to show them that what we do is effective; my experience is that investing in people-focused support will benefit both civilians and responders. If we can end a very sad case with the knowledge that people feel supported and informed in a professional way, this is of huge value. We all know the media headlines of cases where people had a very different experience; this is secondary damage. And if we have to go to court after a complaint is made, we have a situation with just losers—no winners—on a personal level. We can do better, we need to do better, when responding after suicide.

Investigators will want to know when and how the person died. Even if the situation looks like a suicide, it is important to investigate to rule out the involvement of others—maybe even a homicide (covered up to make the situation look like suicide). This is very rare, but it happens.

The investigation may also be, or become, of huge importance to the bereaved. Immediately after the death, there will be acute stress and the situation may feel like absolute chaos. In time, people will start to work through what happened. My experience is that many questions may arise in a later phase. And since the investigators will have noted and filed their findings, many answers may be found in the investigative file.

Tim, 73, who lost his daughter to suicide

The police had told me there was a note, but they advised me not to read it. They said it was an angry note, but didn't share its content with me. After the funeral the thought of the note really started to bother me; What had she written? All kinds of sentences started to pop up in my mind. After a week I decided to contact the detective leading the investigation. He invited me to come over. He first told me what the note had said. And we then watched the note, photographed and opened on a computer screen. It was hard to read it, but I was glad I did.

Sometimes requests or questions will come in a long time after a case has been closed. This can happen because working through grief takes up a lot of time and energy. But there can also be practical reasons—for example, if a parent has died, the child may request information and answers when he or she reaches adulthood. Nowadays filing is mainly done on computers, but there is still a lot of evidence kept in old-fashioned ways.

Supporting James, 13, who lost his father to suicide

James was 13 years old when his father died by suicide. Now, at the age of 18, he was seeing a college psychologist. His father's suicide had posed new questions during therapy sessions. The file from the incident had been stored. James was given access, under the supervision of a detective. With his psychologist present, he asked to see the pictures taken during the incident scene investigation. We put them on the table, upside down. And we put one picture in front of Jim, covered by a piece of paper. James could slide the piece of paper off bit by bit. He did this, going back and forth for a while before he could look at it. He then turned the other pictures over and back, one by one. The detective answered his questions and explained what was in the pictures. It was a relief to James to receive information to provide the missing parts of his memory of that sad day.

Recognize the importance of taking control here: James decided when he was ready to look, step by step, by sliding a piece of paper, by taking the photographs and turning them over to look at them. This was a personal action perspective: he took control; the other people present were facilitating. A very small effort made a huge difference to his experience.

Home invasion

Sarah from the case above found her son in her own house, in his own bedroom. When this happens, a very private space is suddenly taken over by a first-responder invasion.

Take a piece of paper and draw. Alternatively (and even better) see if you can find some Lego® or Playmobil® toys. You may even find a police car and an ambulance around. Now imagine Sarah's house. Draw it or build a scene, using some toys. This may seem silly, but it is important. Think about what would happen in your country, your region, within your protocol. Who would be dispatched? Create a scene and remember that ambulances and police cars are often staffed by multiple people. Put everyone in there—don't forget the coroner or funeral people, or the multiple police teams (in many countries the incident scene will be secured by local police, but scene investigation officers will come in to do the investigation).

Now look at your scene: Sarah, Hannah, and the young boy lived in privacy, until a few hours ago. Look at their street, the vehicles in front of their house. And look at the number of people in there now. If your scene is in a town or city, you could add spectators and maybe even media crowding the street, cameras in hand, opinions ready.

This is a very important part of first-responder training (or at least it should be); take a helicopter view, create an incident map of the situation, and the impact will become much clearer to you.

When responding to a home, remember the impact the first-responder invasion will have on those who are left behind by the deceased. I'll now take you along on a dispatch to a suicide at a home, taken from a blog I wrote a while back.

Suicide at a home

My phone rings. A dispatch. A possible suicide. I get a few details; a home address, a young man, found dead by his mother, the name of the PSNV colleague joining me on this call. He is already driving and will pick me up in three minutes. Local police are on the way, the ambulance and a doctor are almost at the location. I jump into my uniform and get my PSNV-backpack.

When we arrive, the street is busy: several emergency vehicles, many people on the street to watch the spectacle, many of them taking pictures and videos. A reality we face every day. The frantic cries of a woman tell us where we need to go. The doctor steps out and tells the ambulance staff that he won't start CPR.

We go into a house, a safe place, a home... It is now a police scene. We see a mother. Her son went alone. He is gone. Hopelessness. Her home, her privacy. We invade them. The police officers make calls.

Their colleagues from the investigation unit need to come over. This will take a while. The local officers want to secure the evidence. A police scene, many people, many hands and feet. A mother in distress. She sees her child. Wants to hold him.

This was a heartbreaking scene, to the first responders as well. As first responders, we chose our profession because we feel a need to save, to care, to serve. In the past, before PSNV was implemented, emergency doctors often medicated with benzodiazepines in similar situations; utter distress, a police scene—they wanted to help. Trauma science has taught us that this may complicate the situation for the bereaved. So what did PSNV change?

In terms of Maslow's pyramid,[1] during critical incidents we drop down. So we need to start at the first level: safety, security. My colleague looks for a room where we can go. The kitchen is at the back of the house. The audience in the street has no view of it. And it has a door we can close. Psychological alignment. I need to find a way to connect to the mother. So many people around us. I cannot expect her to align to my level of communication. So I find hers. This is the core of what we do. She allows me to put my arm around her. And my colleague and I take her into the kitchen.

Adrenaline, cortisol, fight-flight-freeze mode. Nature has blessed us with a survival mode. Body and brain function changes; cognitive functioning is limited. We need this mode to get through the darkest moments of our lives, but as first responders we need to realize the consequences; we need to adapt, communicate in different ways. Distress is actually a way of coping for the body. People are not ill; they are normal people experiencing normal reactions to an extreme situation.

Most people don't develop pathology. But critical incidents can sometimes lead to serious mental health problems later on. People who experience this tell us that they experienced utter despair, hopelessness, and loss of control during the critical incident.

Back to the mother. Any and every form of control was just taken from her. When she opened the door and saw the worst image a mother can see, her world changed. A long road of grief is ahead of her. There is absolutely nothing we can do to take that away from her. But we can help her toward control. She can't sit down; her body wants to keep

---

1   Psychologist Abraham Maslow described human needs as a hierarchy in the shape of a pyramid, with the most fundamental needs (safety) at the bottom and more sophisticated needs (self-actualization) at the top.

moving. We are in the kitchen. I ask her if it would be possible to make tea. I am not thirsty, but I want to guide her towards ways of functioning. She puts on the kettle.

I start a conversation, using short sentences. Her name. My name. Her son's name. Waves of emotions come and go. We ride them together. I gently ask her about her family. Her son lives with them. Her husband is at work. At the local factory. She is suddenly startled: he doesn't know. My colleague tells her that he will leave the room and talk to the police officers. A duo will drive out to the factory; a police officer and another PSNV colleague will pick up her husband. There is a back entrance to the kitchen. My colleague will instruct them to use it. Is there someone else we need to call? Are there religious rituals we can respect?

Information: What are they doing to my son? When can I see him? Will they take him? I explain the steps taken now. Why are the doctor and the ambulance still here? Why are they taking pictures? I explain about the care they will take. About the coroner, the importance of an investigation. People trained to handle her son with care, just as a normal doctor would examine him. This will take a while. Real information. Honest answers.

My brother died as a baby, after a medical mistake. My mother was not allowed to see or hold him. She was told, "The view will only distress you. It is better that you don't look." Imagine the trauma; our brain fills in the blanks. The image we create is always, always, always worse than the real thing. Putting people in control means that we offer them the option; we never decide for them. Even body parts can be arranged and covered in such a way that a physical goodbye is possible.

My colleague comes back in. He tells us the team is on their way to the husband. Her son (we use his name by now) will be taken by the coroner for further examination. Does she want to see him before he is taken away? A clear "Yes." We decide to wait until the husband arrives.

Now this part of suicide postvention takes some major investing in training and resources. From a police perspective: a body, evidence, an incident scene. So we make sure we respect every technical aspect of their work. But after the on-scene examination, we get to facilitate a moment for the bereaved. Again, only when requested, but our experience is that most bereaved people want to use this. In our backpacks, we carry items to assist us.

Silence. A tremendously important part of our job is to endure silence. Silence can hold so many powerful messages, but it can also hold comfort and peace. Again, as first responders we want to do, to act. In training new colleagues and also from my own experience, I can tell you how difficult it is to endure. And to align. In silence.

Tea. The first adrenaline rush subsides. She is trembling. I can explain this to her; this is completely normal. I tell her I feel so sorry for her loss. I use the name of her son. Is it OK if we talk about him? I adapt to her tense; she uses the present tense so I join her. Tears, but also a proud mother's loving smile when she talks about him. I am a mother myself. This is tough on me. Identification. I make a mental note and will reflect on this during evaluation and team meetings.

The back gate opens. A knock. A colleague tells me the husband is here. A pale-faced man, his shoulders down, walks in. He sits down. Silence. And then the mother is overwhelmed with guilt; she should have known, she should have prevented. He is silent. We let her. We know we need to. Even if we find her arguments irrational, taking on guilt is her way of looking for ways to find control. Reflective listening. No more, no less.

A knock on the other door. The examination is finished. My colleague and a police officer walk in and sit down. We introduce the parents. Condolences are offered. The name of the son is used. The police officer tells the parents that everything seems to confirm that he died by suicide. But the coroner will examine their son and will inform them.

He puts down a folder with paperwork they will need. We will later add specific information from our backpacks; we have many tools and brochures, but will only leave those appropriate in this case: how to deal with the immediate aftermath and information on their local suicide bereavement group. If they want us to, we can arrange contact.

My colleague explains that their son is on a stretcher. How he is covered. There are no injuries visible now, but his skin looks pale with some dark discoloration. My colleague has dimmed the light in the room and he has lit some candles. It is important to describe the image. What will they see? Maybe even feel or smell? They can decide when they are ready. A police officer will be at their side. But they can touch their son's hands and face. That's OK with the police in this case.

In assisting the mother, it is important that we create this image in the room where she found her son. This is her house, her home. We will leave soon, but we don't want to leave this room as the incident scene she saw. She will take control. She will walk back into the room and see a different image. One with dimmed light, candles, and her son.

Control. A very important word. It's an antidote to despair.

They get to say goodbye. As they close the door afterwards, the door towards grief needs to be opened. The long road ahead; everyone is different, the road is personal. But parents who walked the road are available through groups, should they want or need support. Complications may arise: Where can they find helplines and help? Do they want their GP to come over? Is there anyone they want to have around, when we leave?

The mother wants us to call her sister. I sit down with her and I suggest that she makes the call. Takes control. And I will be by her side to support her. She gives me her phone. Her fingers can't manage the touchscreen. But I hand it to her when it dials. My hand is at her shoulder. She makes the call. Lament, tears on the other end. Silence. Her sister's husband will drive her over. She'll be here soon.

The front door is closed. Everyone has left. There are three of us PSNV colleagues now. The sister arrives. Tears, embraces. The GP will visit tomorrow. The local bereavement team will visit the day after. We say our goodbyes. We will probably never see these parents again. We are first responders. We close the front door. We drive over to the police office, have coffee. See if the other first responders need support. Check the ambulance team. If they want us to, we arrange their own peer support teams to take over; support in the same uniform works best.

I get home. Take off my uniform, my backpack. I take a shower and join my own world, where everything is normal. I live in the mountains, watch my kids do normal stuff, hang out with my animals. And I count my blessings; life is fragile.

This is typical of calls our teams get on a daily basis. Most team members work a few shifts a month and have another day job, mostly in first response or healing professions. On average, a suicide postvention call will take about four hours from dispatch to closing, but there is no strict timeline we follow.

Key factors during the response were:

- practicing psychological alignment

- mitigating feelings of hopelessness and helplessness by finding ways to resume control

- structuring and supporting the multidisciplinary response.

Found by a stranger

Sometimes a body is found by a stranger. When someone ends their life, many life lines are brought together; a body will be found and first responders will be called. Over the years I have learned not to make assumptions about how a situation may or may not affect someone. Finding a body may disturb and even traumatize some; others may make some calls and experience less of an impact on their personal situation. There is no right or wrong and no way to prepare a standard response to support people in this situation.

We know a situation may be disturbing if we experience a high level of identification with the situation and/or the deceased. But the most important advice I want to give you is not to assume but check; assess the situation and practice psychological alignment; find the person you want to attend to where *they* are. Even if a scene looks very disturbing to you, never assume, but look at the person encountering the situation and work from there. I will give you an example of two people confronted with the same situation:

Gemma, 48, and Paul, 58

Gemma

I walk my dog a few times a day and I try to change routes once in a while. That morning my dog ran into a bush in the forest and did not return. I called for him and knew something was wrong when he did not obey, but started to bark. I knew a search for a missing person was being done in the area and I got a strange feeling. I kept calling my dog and he continued to bark, so I started to carefully make my way over to see what had caught his attention. I immediately saw that the young man behind the bush had been dead for a while. This must be the young boy I had seen on the missing person's flyers. I work at a home for the elderly and I am familiar with dead bodies. I felt sad for his loved ones. I put the dog on the leash and took out my phone to call the emergency number. A jogger came over, because he had heard the dog. He got very upset and I stayed with him until the police arrived. It was a very sad ending to a search they had conducted over the past few days. But the uncertainty must have been awful for the boy's relatives. I hope they have found closure. Someone had to find the boy. I guess fate decided I had to be that person that day. It reminded me of how fragile life can be. And I count my own blessings more often now.

Paul

I was jogging as I usually do, but I took a shortcut through the forest that day. I heard a dog bark and a lady calling, so I went to see if she needed help. I will never forget what I saw when I got to them; I first saw his shoes. They were the same kind I had just bought for my son. I was breathing fast, because I had run over quickly, but it felt like my heart exploded in my chest. I saw a horrible scene, one I had never seen before. A young boy had died and he had been dead for a while. This was someone's son; my son was about the same age. I got extremely upset and I don't really remember what happened next. The lady had called the police and I was taken home. That night I could not sleep and this image of the boy and the shoes kept appearing, causing panic. I thought I was going crazy; I did not even know the boy who had died! I started to drink before going to sleep, which did not help. My wife made me see my GP. I asked him for sleep medication, but he referred me to a therapist. I had never seen one before, but I was desperate, so I went. I received sessions of EMDR,[2] and the image is no longer appearing and messing up my life. I will never forget what I saw, but the treatment has helped me to look at it as a horrible memory. I can control it now and I can talk about it now.

Gemma and Paul objectively encountered the same situation, but their subjective way of coping with it was completely different. Gemma's way of coping was very productive: she leashed her dog, alerted emergency services, and protected the incident scene. Supporting Paul gave her an extra action perspective. It's important to facilitate productive coping; Gemma did not need any support and she was able to mentally frame the situation and move on with her day-to-day activities. Paul experienced a completely different situation: he identified with the situation—this could have been his son. He needed some professional support to help him return to healthy day-to-day functioning.

---

2   Eye movement desensitization and reprocessing, a therapy for post-traumatic stress.

Eustress, distress, and dysfunction

Every time we start training new colleagues, we ask them how they define stress, so I want to ask you: What is stress to you? How do you define it?

Stress nowadays has a very negative image in society. So I bet many of your comments and answers would view stress as something impacting us in negative ways.

In crisis intervention we actually look at stress from a neutral perspective. We use the definition that endocrinologist Hans Selye gave us in 1936: *stress is the non-specific response of the body to any demand for change.* My translation: *stress is any response to any trigger (stressor).*

In the Introduction, I wrote about what happens when our lives are threatened; we go into survival mode, also called flight–fight–freeze mode. Evolution left us this quick-response mode, and it can actually help us survive when action and reaction are needed. When stressors trigger us, our body and mind respond; stressors may cause our bodies to respond in similar ways, but our mind may interpret a situation in a different way. This is part of our way of coping with life and situations, and it is different in each one of us; we have all experienced different life events and our brains have all developed in different ways.

Let me give you a classic example. Imagine taking a rollercoaster ride. One person will get very excited and happy by just thinking about it. Another will immediately get scared and upset by just thinking about it. If I put both of them in the same rollercoaster, their bodies will experience similar G-force and movement. Adrenaline will be secreted, and the body will respond to that by increasing blood pressure, sweating, and other physical stress responses. While their physical responses will be similar, their experience of the ride will be completely different; one will enjoy the ride and jump out, laughing, saying, "Wow, awesome! I want to ride again!" This person is experiencing what we call *eustress*. The second person will be disturbed, frightened, and will crawl out, saying, "Never again! That was horrible." This person is experiencing what we call *distress*.

The *stressor* in both people (the rollercoaster ride) is the same. The *physical stress* (the response) in both people is similar. The *psychological effect*, however, is very different and subjective; they will experience, interpret, validate, and frame the situation in very different ways. There is no *good* or *bad* label to be handed out here; the way we interpret situations is a result of our personal life journey.

Now back to our scene. Gemma and Paul both encountered the same situation; both experienced a physical stress response. But Gemma's subjective experience was a completely different one to Paul's. This is what we see during and after critical incidents. Gemma experienced *eustress*; she immediately found action perspectives. Paul experienced *distress*; he experienced severe reactions and got upset. He identified with the situation and needed some support to get home and to work through what had happened; he experienced *dysfunction*.

Group dynamics

When managing an incident, as a first responder, it can be very helpful to look at reactions from a group dynamics perspective. Especially when a group of people is directly affected, it may be complicated to control a situation.

After a critical incident, people all experience a huge amount of physical stress and are in an adrenaline rush, but their experiences and reactions differ. There is a lot of energy surrounding a scene, and some of it can be very helpful; people in *eustress* tend to be the helpers; they need action perspectives. When they are blocked from following up on them, you may encounter a huge adrenaline-based aggression potential (remember Sarah at the beginning of this chapter?). You will also encounter people in *distress* in your group; they may be very upset, screaming, crying, acting out in other emotional ways. These are normal reactions of people reacting to an extreme situation. It's just the way their body and mind respond to a huge amount of stress hormones; they are not ill or experiencing "symptoms."

My own experience has taught me that it is very helpful to learn about different kinds of reactions and group dynamics, and actively work with them during and after a critical incident. How does that work? What do you do?

People in eustress need action perspectives; they want to get busy, to get moving, to get helping. People in distress need a safe place, guidance, and action perspectives to help them cope with the situation. There's your answer—one group of people can support the other. You just need to specify some action perspectives and facilitate the process and you will see some amazing results.

A huge benefit of working in this way is that you will stay available for the group of people experiencing immediate dysfunction. In very rare cases, people will need immediate physical or mental healthcare. This will only apply to a small number of people. In some cases you will not even encounter it, but it is important to be aware and available. When in doubt about a person's mental or physical reactions and health, don't hesitate to refer them and get them immediate professional help or safety.

Aligning in silence

When looking at responses within your group, you will also encounter a different kind of dysfunction; people may get stuck in the *freeze* part of the fight–flight–freeze mode. These people need support, but they are often overlooked in modern society; the reality is that those who are loudest will generally be attended to first. But they are often not those who need the most urgent help.

If you are a medical professional, you'll understand what I mean because you know how to triage; the patients who are very vocal and voicing their needs may not be the ones needing the most urgent medical attention; if someone is running around and screaming, you can be reassured that their heart is beating and that they are breathing just fine. During and after critical incidents the same principle may apply, if you look at them from our crisis intervention perspective.

Some people may experience what we call *tonic immobility*; they will not be able to move their body or parts of their body under extreme stress. And some people may not respond to you at all. These people need support. Always remember this, even when surrounded by a huge amount of distress responses in others: *Don't miss the silent and quiet people.*

Some may tell you they want to be left alone; that is a great response, and you should respect their wishes. But if you notice there is no response, offer immediate support. Make sure the person who will be offering support can be available for a while, because time is what will probably be needed.

Petra, crisis intervention volunteer

We were called to a railway suicide at the train station. Many people had seen what had happened, so the two colleagues who arrived first upscaled the incident and more of us were dispatched. I was asked to support a young woman. She was sitting on a bench in a small waiting booth near the platform. There was a lot of noise around her: first responders tending to the young man on the tracks, police officers looking for information and securing evidence, many upset witnesses, and even more nosy people, including some journalists. I tried to align to the young woman by sitting down next to her, speaking in a slow and calm voice. My aim was to get her away from there and find a quiet room to support her. I could not get any response, so I asked a police officer to clear the waiting room, close the door, and make sure nobody could come in. I pointed out to him the media representatives and the vulnerability of this young woman. He promised to keep an eye on our privacy, which turned out to be of no concern; the onlookers were only interested in the scene on the tracks.

When the door was closed, the sound level was much lower. I sat down next to the young woman and introduced myself: "My name is Petra. I am a member of the crisis intervention team and I would like to sit with you for a while. Would that be OK?" No response.

This is where our training comes in; we are trained to endure the silence some people may need. This is a very difficult part of our job, and I had never realized this before I started this volunteer work. I sat down close to the young woman, but I left her plenty of personal space; she could not set boundaries. I made sure I did not touch her.

So we sat together. I wanted to find openings to align to her. Psychological alignment is about so much more than words. I copied her body position and tried to look in the direction of whatever her gaze was fixed on. After a few minutes in this more secure situation (door closed, sound level down), her breathing became less shallow.

She took some deep breaths. I used my calmest voice and said: "I am so very sorry we need to meet in these conditions. I don't even know your name. My name is Petra; could you tell me yours?"

Her body relaxed a little and she looked at me. This is a very important moment when offering support in such a situation; if someone offers you eye contact, they are offering you a huge opening. But you need to catch it. I did. She told me her name and took a deep breath. The two of us had connected.

She allowed me to stay with her until she felt well enough to be driven home, where we could find safety and privacy for her. Once there, we had a long talk; she had lost a friend to suicide and watching what happened that morning triggered many memories. She was seeing a therapist once every six weeks, so we both agreed it would be a good idea to call him and ask for an extra appointment.

The young woman had a good cry and we drank strong tea together. I spent about three hours in total with her. Before returning home, I met my team colleagues and we had coffee together at the police station. We spoke about the incident and made sure everyone on the team was OK. As with any case, this case was later discussed in our monthly team meeting.

Again, always look out for the quiet people, as they are often overlooked. They may be fine and tell you so—that's great! Others will need you. Make sure you see them!

Here is a case example involving a large group of people. I have chosen a school setting, but many of the aspects could be translated to other group settings (workplaces, public areas, etc.).

A school setting

The second period had just started when several students, seated at window tables, saw a shadow passing their window. They jumped up and looked down. On the asphalt they saw a body, face down. There was no movement and they did not recognize who was down there, but their art teacher had just jumped from the roof of the school and died.

This is a situation we have sadly encountered multiple times over the years. In some cases, teachers, in others, students, died by suicide during school hours. A situation like this has a tremendous impact on hundreds of people; the loved ones of the deceased, colleagues, and classmates. But everyone at school and every parent at home is affected in some way by the suicide. The media will cover the incident—often helped by social media, because every student can become an instant reporter by taking their cellphone out and going online.

Sometimes first aid and/or CPR may be attempted. Every school has a system and trained people available to do this. Within the same system, emergency services will be informed and they will quickly be dispatched. Parts of the school grounds and the roof will become a police scene and an investigation will follow.

Two major challenges have just arisen:

- A very disturbing event just took place (trauma aspects).

- Someone everyone knew suddenly died (grief aspects).

It's very important to keep both aspects in mind amidst all the complexity this incident poses. In a school or work setting, both aspects will be prominent. If a suicide is witnessed by strangers, in a public area, the first aspect will be more prominent; every case is different, so you will not find "perfect response plans" in this book. A suicide will cause crisis in general and multiple crises for those it affects.

Back to school. This is a very complicated situation. Every school will have crisis protocols; work with what is available. Ask for the crisis protocol and make sure it is activated. Many schools are very experienced and used to regular drills and scenario exercises. Only add what is needed: *if a system, a team, or a person is functioning well, let them function!* Facilitate and make sure their action perspective is not interrupted.

The crisis protocol will state who will be leading and who will be communicating in the case of an emergency. If they are doing so, let them. If people need support, help them to find their designated action perspective. Or help them delegate if this is not possible.

Suicide postvention, as implemented within crisis intervention, will focus on supporting the organization and the first responders through the first aspect of what happened; the death was very sudden and witnessed by several young people. The primary damage (the death of a teacher) can't be reversed. But we will put in our best efforts to help prevent secondary damage and possible trauma.

Then there is the grief aspect in this case; when the initial chaos has subsided and the first response finished, the school will have to work through grief and loss. Most schools will have protocols to support them. And school psychologists, social workers, and pastoral care will be available in most countries, implemented in emergency plans.

While providing suicide postvention, we will ask about grief protocols, plans, and people that we can activate to support the school; again, always check what is there already before adding any external services. My experience is that schools can manage grief and loss aspects very well with their existing support system. We leave links to organizations they can contact if more expertise is needed.

Now, back to the crisis aspect in this incident; remember our definition of crisis? It is the *reaction* to the incident, *not* the incident itself. So in this case we have a suicide (technically a sudden death that needs to be investigated). The chaos and disorganization that may follow is the crisis we respond to. In a similar case, we have seen a lot of secondary damage when well-meant advice had unintended consequences.

A school setting, unintended consequences

The school secretary was enjoying a quiet day at the office because the principal was away for training. Suddenly, two students entered her office, crying and talking in an incomprehensible way. They told her that someone had fallen off the roof and she needed to call the emergency number. Their teacher had gone out to give first aid, but they said the man had not moved since he fell on the concrete and there was blood coming from his head.

The secretary asked them where the man was and immediately called the emergency number, but she did not know what to do next. She realized that many of the classrooms had a view of where he was, and she did not want students to see what was going on. So she went to the school speaker microphone and made an announcement: "Teachers in the classrooms at the entrance side of the school, please keep your students away from the windows."

Consequently, and unfortunately, the teenagers in the classrooms reacted as teenagers do: they all got up and wanted to see what was going on outside. Students currently not in class went outside and were confronted with a horrific scene and panicking teachers.

Although this secretary had the best intentions, her actions had the opposite effect: well meant is not always well done.

Here's what another secretary did. I have repeated the first part.

A school setting, making the best decision under the circumstances

The school secretary was enjoying a quiet day at the office because the principal was away for training. Suddenly, two students entered her office, crying and talking in an incomprehensible way. They told her that someone had fallen off the roof and she needed to call the emergency number. Their teacher had gone out to give first aid, but they said the man had not moved since he fell on the concrete and there was blood coming from his head.

The secretary asked them where the man was and immediately called the emergency number, but she did not know what to do next. She realized that many of the classrooms had a view of where he was, and she did not want students to see what was going on. She knew the fire drill plans. The incident happened at the entrance side of the school. During a fire drill the students would evacuate and gather at the back of the school, on the soccer field. The students were very familiar with practicing at unexpected times.

She activated the school fire alarm, as she would do during a drill. She then sat down and made the announcements she needed to make through the speaker phone in case of an evacuation. She asked the students in her office to sit down for a few minutes. She could see the students walking out calmly, as they had to do so often. After the evacuation, she walked the two students to the soccer field, where they joined their classmates. Two teachers had already taken charge and in the background she could hear the sirens indicating that the emergency services had arrived.

Same situation, different responses. But these are just two examples; there is no "perfect response" to any critical incident. The secretary in the second example made the best decision possible under the circumstances she was confronted with; the students evacuated calmly.

There are many more possible scenarios. Some schools have blinds that could be closed to block the view. Students could stay in their classrooms and only those classes with a view of what happened need immediate information on how to proceed; others won't have noticed and classes could continue. Since sirens will be approaching soon, a speaker announcement could be made. For example:

Dear students and teachers, someone was seriously injured after a fall on school grounds. The school nurse and other staff members are offering first aid, but you will soon hear emergency services arriving because we called for help. Students and teachers, you can assist us and them by remaining in your classrooms. Please continue classes. As soon as we receive more information, we will pass it on to you.

This would help to contain the situation very quickly; *heterogeneous* and *homogeneous* groups (see below) are already separated—helpful from our crisis intervention perspective, but also from an investigative point of view, should the police need information from those who witnessed what happened. Within the classrooms, you could later differentiate further. Here is why.

When we arrive on scene, we will immediately start asking one simple question: *Who saw what happened?* We will separate the (few) students who did from the rest of the group. Since we don't know what happened, there is an important security aspect connected to this question; a sudden death may sometimes turn out to be a homicide and a suspect may be on the run. Our question will assist the police in gaining information quickly.

From our crisis intervention perspective, the question is important because we know that experiences shared can really upset others who did not experience them first-hand. This may even lead to what we call secondary trauma (also known as vicarious trauma). This is a severe complication; most people will not develop psychopathology (mental illness), but separating people on the basis of their experience will help to prevent it; a terrible incident has occurred, adrenaline is up, and witnesses may tell very vivid stories, describing what they saw. Others may take on these images and be disturbed by them. A colleague who suffered secondary trauma calls this "secondhand trauma." It is not an official term, but I think it is spot on.

Heterogeneous and homogeneous groups

If you look at this incident (let's imagine the evacuation scenario), you will now envision all the students and teachers together on the soccer field; everyone who was in the school building, all together. This is a *heterogeneous* group. Then we come in and ask our question: *Who saw what happened?* If we take the students (and maybe some teachers) and separate them from the others, we have created a *homogeneous* group: they share an experience—they all witnessed the teacher fall or they saw him motionless in a pool of blood.

Homogeneous groups can also be formed using many other criteria, asking a different question; the teacher may have been mentor to a specific group of children or to a specific class. They are/feel close to him. You may look at the teachers at school as a homogeneous group; they are his peers, his direct colleagues. Or there may be an art department at school that connects a certain group of people here.

Later, homogeneous groups will come together while working through the *grief and loss aspects* of the death. But we are supporting to limit or prevent secondary damage through *traumatization*. So we will form a homogeneous group by asking a simple but important question: *Who saw what happened?* By separating the homogeneous group from the heterogeneous group, we prevent distress (potentially secondary trauma) in those who did not see what happened. We have the opportunity to inform them about what happened in a safe and controlled way.

Meanwhile, we have the opportunity to immediately support those who saw the disturbing scene. This is a relatively small group of people—in this case, a group of teenagers. Teenagers are brilliant peer supporters if we facilitate them.

Experience has taught us that these small groups find comfort and support in each other's presence; we will be with them and align with their needs. Sometimes someone may need one-on-one support. Just make sure that is available, but only offer it when needed. Don't force people to sit down in a one-on-one talk just because the protocol tells you to do so. Needs are very personal; some witnesses will want to talk, but others won't. Walk alongside; don't push or pull.

Police officers are trained to collect information. They will only question those able to give answers and only when they need to, because that is what the situation requires them to do.

Keeping control of the message

When I trained as a psychiatric nurse we didn't have cellphones, but nowadays news is brought right into our hands. And it travels fast. Media instructions are a huge part of our response. If the school crisis protocol covers the "phone issue," then implement that. My experience is that this is not always an option.

Here are some of the choices I have made. They may not work for everyone. I just want to share them as possible options. I am not in favor of forbidding people to use their phones; if you know young people, you will know what will happen. Instead, I give very clear instructions, which kids experiencing increased adrenaline will follow (again, that is my experience). The school could post a message on the school's website and social media channels. An example of spoken instruction to students would be:

Listen, we are still awaiting information and there are many questions we can't answer yet. But this is a serious situation and it would be very helpful if you would send your parents a message. Let them know you are safe. Tell them someone was seriously injured (or someone has died) after a fall on school grounds. Emergency services are here and asking parents to stay at home, so they have room to help. Please ask your parents to watch the school website for information.

Make sure the message on the school website matches the wording and tone you use while instructing the students. In countries where there are regular threats to schools, you may add a clear message: there is no danger or threat to the school, all children and teachers are safe and supported.

When incidents happen, we go out to find information. Nowadays, we search online. Everyone owning a cellphone can become a reporter. Even if there is not much to share yet, make sure you offer information. Provide updates and make sure the underlying message is "We don't have answers or details, but we will share them as soon as we receive them."

If fake news is being spread, it may be good to answer it with facts, but make sure that they are verified before sharing them. The human mind under stress will be looking for information and answers. If they are not found, they will be made up and blanks will be filled. More on this in later chapters.

When there is no body

Mary, 48, whose husband was never found

My husband had been at work that day. I had cooked dinner after his shift ended, but he didn't come home. I tried to call him, but his phone was off. I assumed his battery was dead, so I called his workplace. His colleague said he had left as usual and I got worried; he must have been involved in a traffic incident. I called the police to ask them if anything had happened. They asked me for details about his route and told me the roads were clear and no incidents had been reported. I left my phone number and my husband's name, cellphone number, and license plate. It was too early to file a missing person's report, they said. "Husbands sometimes take unplanned detours," the officer on the phone said. He thought it was quite funny. I didn't. So I waited, but I was extremely worried.

Sometimes people are reported missing. Their loved ones may be extremely worried about their wellbeing, expecting something bad to have happened. Others may simply not have had a clue about what happened: nothing was out of the ordinary; as far as they could see, their loved one just suddenly disappeared. Sometimes it may take a while for such cases to be reported.

When people are reported missing, most of them will return home safely. This is important to note, and the officer in Mary's story (above) probably assumed Mary's missing husband was one of those cases. Unfortunately, it turned out to be different, and Mary felt as if he hadn't taken her seriously. Words matter. And reassurance is great, but it has to find its recipient, not miss it. Well meant is not always well done. The psychological alignment between Mary and this officer did not click during their conversation.

Mary continued

The next day my doorbell rang. When I peered outside, I saw a police car and I thought I would faint; something had happened and they had found him. I stumbled to the door. One of the officers introduced himself as the person I spoke to yesterday, when I called the police station. I asked if they had found him. I was breathing very fast. I just had to know. The other officer immediately said, "No, we did not find your husband, but..." I don't remember what followed, because my knees wobbled and I almost fell down.

We sat down and he told me again; my husband had not been found. But...they had found his car and that was what worried them. The car had been found near the highway bridge. The spot was known as a "hotspot," where several people had ended their lives lately. A commuter had called in yesterday afternoon, because he had seen a man, walking near the highway. His description matched my husband's.

I got very upset and angry; what were they saying? That they expected my husband had jumped off the bridge? That was absolutely ridiculous! We had been married for so many years, talked about difficult stuff; my husband would never ever leave me like that!

The officers clearly did not know what to say. They asked if there was someone they could call to stay with me, but I just wanted them to leave. Oh, the anger I felt! I told them to get out and look for my husband. He must have been involved in something else on that highway.

This is a heartbreaking situation. Putting all the information together, the officers are worried that a life has been lost to suicide, but Mary hasn't lost hope.

Mary continued

The police car drove away. I turned on the computer and started my search browser. This could not be; I needed answers. What was I looking for? I didn't know where to start. I typed in words about my situation and I suddenly found a story of a man who had been missing for years. Nobody knew what had happened to him, but he had hitchhiked his way through the country after he suffered total memory loss. He was offered support by a charity and they helped him to find a job. Years later his desperate family went to a TV show broadcast to give attention to missing person's cases. His neighbor saw and recognized the man's photograph, and he was reunited with his family.

This. This. This. This was what had happened to my husband too! The highway, hitchhiking, it all made sense! I needed to get out his picture; he was out there, all alone, and probably needed help. But where to begin? My anxiety calmed down; the police officers were wrong. And I would find him.

Mary went on an internet search and found this miraculous story of someone being reunited with loved ones years after they went missing. Hope picks up these stories and composes a theory of what might have happened. It's a coping strategy, a structure to hold on to—mind over matter. Mary had built a structure to hold on to her hope. It gave her a lifeline to grab on to. In Chapter 5 you will read more about this, as taking on guilt is a very similar phenomenon.

Mary continued—Jim, police officer

My partner and I were both silent in the car on our way back to the police station. We had been with the wife of a missing person. His car had been found at the location that had recently become a hotspot; several people had taken their lives by jumping off the highway bridge. Our colleagues recognized the license plate because I had put it in the notification system a few hours earlier, just in case. They went to have a closer look and found the car open. The car keys, an ID and a wallet were on the driver's seat. They looked untouched by others, as if they had been put there with care.

No other clues and no farewell note were found in the car. But the discovery was worrying, especially since a call had come in reporting a man walking by the highway. Another patrol car had driven past, but they saw no one.

We had planned to inform the wife in person about all the details, but she seemed to assume we came to tell her we had found her missing husband. There was no real conversation and she got extremely upset with us when we told her why we were very worried. We offered to call someone to stay with her, but she just wanted us to leave.

What could we have done? What should we have done? The home visit certainly did not go as planned. How to proceed now? We both didn't know what to say while driving back. I was replaying all the steps we took, all the words that were spoken in my mind. And I just felt awful.

This situation escalated and the fact is that these situations will occur and can't always be prevented; this is an extreme situation for Mary. Her way of reacting to it is an effort to deal with what is going on; missing a loved one causes tremendous feelings of hopelessness and powerlessness. Her aggression is a way (for Mary) to try to (re)gain control over all these chaotic and horrific feelings.

This happens. I have had people hit me with their fists, watched doors being kicked out, and seen plates and cups fly. It is very important to remember that this aggression is not aimed at you, it is aimed at the situation. But it can be very harmful. Safety should always be our first concern, and in extreme cases we (temporarily) need to provide safety measures when people are at immediate risk of harming themselves or others.

If this case had been from a country where we go out with officers as a crisis intervention team, we might have been able to help as a third mediating party; de-escalating in this situation without a police officer's badge and uniform may have given us an advantage.

Maybe Mary would have listened, but looking back in hindsight is always easy; the reality might have been different. What we would have done for sure is support these officers afterwards. Having been with them, this would be a natural follow up, since we could all reflect on what happened from a "we-perspective."

These cases are very tough on officers. Most people think about shooting sprees and car chases when we talk about tough police stuff. But believe me when I tell you that the situation above would make an officer's classified tough-stuff list. If Mary's husband had been found dead and they'd had to inform her, the case would still make the same list.

As a daughter, granddaughter, and colleague of police officers for many, many years, I have never met an officer who got used to these situations or who felt they were easy to respond to. Yes, the police profession was their choice and, yes, everyone knows that these cases come with the job, but they are heavy on all of us as first responders.

Since this book is about the immediate response after suicide, I will give only some brief details about how Mary's situation developed. She allowed her local chaplain to support her and found strength in her faith. Mary and her chaplain made an appointment with the officers who found her husband's car. She was allowed to look at the pictures taken and saw how her husband's personal belongings had been found on his car seat. It was hard to look at them, but it helped Mary to come to terms with the situation. She was also shown a transcript of the call a driver had made, informing the police about a man walking next to the highway near the bridge.

A week later, Mary, the chaplain, and a police officer drove out to the location. It was the last known location her husband had visited and being there was very emotional for Mary. The chaplain and the police officer planned a lot of time for this visit and Mary needed that. They walked out onto the bridge together, and, as Mary looked down, she realized that nobody would survive a fall from there. The chaplain had brought a rose and said a prayer. Although closure was not possible and Mary still had some hope and doubt left, this ritual helped her.

She started to see a therapist and gradually found peace and calmness. A long process of working through legal aspects would follow. A victim support organization helped her. Mary's future as she had hoped and dreamed it was lost the day her husband disappeared. She is still grieving and working through the many difficult aspects of what happened to her.

CHAPTER 1—SUMMARY

- When a body is discovered, emergency services will respond.

- The location of the body will become a police scene. Depending on where the body is found, this may lead to a huge invasion of privacy. It is important to explain to people who will respond, what they will need to do, and why this is important.

- Action perspectives and ways of taking control can be an antidote to feelings of helplessness and hopelessness. Look for ways to facilitate this.

- Sometimes lifesaving attempts may need to be stopped. If CPR has been started by civilians, this situation will need to be handled with empathy and care.

- After suicide, a medical professional will report that the death was not caused by natural causes. An investigation of the body and the circumstances surrounding the death will follow.

- Although investigators may suspect that someone died by suicide, we are officially not responding to a suicide but to a sudden death that needs to be investigated.

- Before the cause of death can be officially established as a suicide, investigators will investigate who died, when they died, and how they died.

- In England and Wales, a public coroner's inquest will be held to review the investigative evidence and determine the cause of death. It is important to inform yourself about the rules and regulations in your own country, as they will differ.

- Everyone reacts differently when confronted with sudden death or a dead body. People confronted with the same situation and images may respond in very different ways.

- Don't assume; always work in psychological alignment.

- People may experience reactions to acute stress.

- People experiencing eustress may need action perspectives.

- People experiencing distress may need guidance and peer support in a safe environment.

- People experiencing dysfunction may need more support and assistance. On rare occasions, immediate referral to professional health-care may be required.

- If suicide occurs in a large group setting, such as a school or a company, crisis management plans will be available. Work with what and with whom you find available. Don't add more than necessary.

- Grief aspects will need to be addressed during the aftermath.

- Trauma aspects need your attention during the response; a risk of secondary trauma may be present.

- Working with homogeneous and heterogeneous groups will limit risks.

- Action perspectives and ways of taking control can be an antidote to feelings of helplessness and hopelessness.

- When there is a suspicion of suicide but no body is found, this poses a very difficult situation to the people missing a loved one.

- Working on these missing person's cases is very demanding on first responders.

- Questions and conflict may arise. Transparent information and the implementation of rituals may help.

2

Breaking the Bad News

This chapter will give you step-by-step guidance on how to inform the bereaved after a sudden death, possibly a suicide. This is a very demanding part of police work. I will show you how, we as crisis interventionists, support officers while delivering death notifications, and how this message can be delivered in a safe and professional way.

A police officer's duty will in many cases not be limited to informing the next of kin of the deceased; an incident scene needs to be secured, an investigation needs to be done. In countries where we go out with the police, we can pre-plan different responsibilities and roles, which works very well. We usually meet at the police station and drive over together. I can't copy and paste these kinds of services to your country. Work with whomever and whatever you have available. And even if you have to go out on your own, see what you can implement.

When starting a career at the police academy, many future officers don't really think about this demanding part of police work. In most countries, it's a legal obligation that one close relative is informed by the police after a sudden death.

A suicide is a sudden death, and it is important to know that the investigation into the death will probably still be ongoing when the bereaved are informed. Sometimes the evidence base is very clear, and a police officer may be able to say, "We believe your loved one died by suicide." In other cases this may not be verified information.

It is very important to keep in mind that the police are always in the lead here; there is an active police scene and an active ongoing (criminal) investigation. These aspects need to be respected.

A note for police managers

If you are in police management and reading this, please implement this part of the job into continued education. We see that it is rarely done; police officers receive a lot of ongoing training, but this intervention is often left out. The reality is that every police officer will have to go out on this task, and we know how the wellbeing and self-confidence of police staff, as well as the quality of the service delivered in these cases, increases after we train officers.

You don't need any materials to train or practice this; just a confidential and safe setting and an open mindset. Please consider adding the (very short) scenario "establishing contact and delivering the death notification" to your curricula.

In Germany we, as the PSNV (Psychosocial Emergency Service), join the police whenever this is possible. We meet up and drive over together. The police officer will perform his duty and deliver the message. Often investigative tasks will need to follow, as they are a part of police work. The officer can focus on his tasks, and we are there to offer emergency support.

Although the police could just inform one person and leave the rest to the family, we feel this is not always enough; we often see what is nowadays called "patchwork structuring" within families—"next of kin" doesn't always mean those closest to them.

Often children live with different (step)parents, sometimes far away. We then set up a dispatch in the city of residence of the bereaved child (there's 24/7 national coverage in Germany); a local police officer and a PSNV colleague will make sure the child is informed in cooperation with his or her caregivers (depending on the age of the child).

We feel it is not up to us to judge, to comment on, or to intervene in family situations in any way. But we feel every child has the right to be informed and supported when a parent dies. And every child has the right to be supported when someone near and dear to them dies.

Who to inform?

Nowadays, people live in many different social and family arrangements. Almost a century ago, when my grandfather became a police officer, people lived in more traditional family structures. Informing next of kin was less complicated then, and news didn't travel as fast as it does now. Now we have the freedom to find love and live our lives the way we choose. This is wonderful, but it can complicate a situation after a sudden death: those legally entitled to be informed as next of kin may not be the ones the deceased was closest to.

When there is a death, and especially when a death is completely unexpected, we encounter situations where decisions surrounding death have never been discussed. There are no plans made for all the necessary arrangements. If there are no legal documents describing the wishes of the deceased, his or her next of kin will be those who will be informed and allowed to make decisions, even if others were much closer to the person.

When children are in the picture, this can lead to dramatic situations (and I am not exaggerating). It is very important to keep professional boundaries in our work; as first responders, we are involved in a case for just a few hours. We can refer, but it is not up to us to take on more than crisis intervention has to offer. Legally, the police only need to inform one next of kin after a sudden death. In areas where our crisis intervention teams work, we sometimes make an exception; when we encounter situations where children are bereaved and lose a direct family member, we always try to find a way to inform them. There is no legal obligation for us to do so, but we all agree that every child deserves our support as the impact of suicide is so massive. Since we have national 24/7 coverage in Germany, we can offer this; even if children or siblings live far away, a police officer and a colleague will go out to inform the child.

Many questions (and even some concerns) may arise while you're reading this, and there's enough to comment on for a whole new book, but I won't go into further depth here.

How to inform next of kin after a sudden death

Verify

Make sure you are informed as accurately as possible. Check names and information, and read names a few times; there is no room for trial and error when informing the bereaved. Inform yourself on the investigation, which is probably still ongoing.

Don't delay

We live in a digital age; social media travels faster than we ever will. Sometimes people will receive messages before we can get to them. In some countries (the Netherlands, for example), first-responder dispatch information is shared on social media. When a body is found, Twitter will know. This is a reality. And it can complicate our work.

Prepare, but don't waste any time. You are about to go out on a difficult job; get to it as soon as you can.

Team up

Who will go out? I would consider going out in tandem; a difficult job is best done together. I know this is not always possible, but I always recommend working in a team and we try to make sure new colleagues team up with an experienced officer.

Prepare

While on the way, discuss the steps you will take: who will speak the words, give the message, etc. It helps to do this in advance, and maybe even to decide on the exact words together.

Sometimes we see police officers preparing in an almost protocol-like way. If this helps, do so, but remember that every human being is different. There is no way to predict how the people you are about to meet will respond to two police officers suddenly showing up. Make sure there is flexibility in your planning to adapt to the situation as it develops.

Support each other

It will be a tough drive; you are about to invade the privacy of people and deliver them the worst message they will ever receive. And you know it. Please know that the person sitting next to you is experiencing the same situation. I have not met one police officer who feels this part of the job gets easier through the years.

You know yourself and you probably know your fellow officer; use your own coping strategies, whatever works for you. You are about to see real people and real emotions in an extremely vulnerable situation. But you will be with them. Without getting spiritual here, there is a ministry of presence we can offer in this situation; by being there, voicing transparent, honest, information in a professional and compassionate way, you are offering them a tremendous service. There is no perfection in being human, but it is of huge value.

A two-phase procedure

Cindy, 58, who lost her husband to suicide

I was not even dressed, wearing my bathrobe over my nightgown, my feet in slippers. I don't even remember how many people were in the house; the situation was completely overwhelming me. I felt like I had been thrown out of an airplane without a parachute; I really was in free fall. I was told to stay in the kitchen while they were investigating my husband's body in the stairwell. I was not allowed to go out there. I am sure they worked as fast as they could, but in my memory I was in there for ages.

Included in the Introduction was a little on how trauma works and how we use action perspectives and taking control as an antidote in situations of helplessness and hopelessness. The fact is that we, as responders, have to take control after a suicide. First, to take control of the location where the body was found, but also when we are informing the bereaved; there is no way to predict how people will react, so we need to create a situation where we can inform them in privacy. In addition, there may be investigative questions that need to be answered, evidence to be collected, or identification to be requested.

Remember, at this early stage we are not talking about suicide as a cause of death established after an investigation; we are responding to a sudden death. Sometimes it is possible to explain it as a suspected suicide; in other cases, we will have to tell people we just don't know what happened yet. Whatever the circumstances you are working with, I have found that the whole procedure of informing next of kin consists of two phases. The first phase of your intervention is what I call the *directive phase*; the second I call the *support phase.*

The directive phase

As you can see from the scenario earlier in this chapter, you start off in a very directive way; there is a legal obligation to inform, but many human aspects are involved. People's privacy is at stake, and we overwhelm them when we march into their houses with a message that will change their world forever. Until the information is given and investigative tasks are done, you take control of the situation as police officers. Your intervention starts as soon as you enter the surroundings of the people you are going to inform; you will probably enter their street in uniform, in a police car.

Be aware of your visibility; you will draw attention and people will come out to watch you. Some may get anxious, others just very curious. You are not out on patrol; you are out on a specific and complicated mission. Don't get distracted, stay focused, and make sure your body language and attitude match the task. Keep your eyes and ears open when you get to the house you will be visiting; look out for clues, but never automatically assume. If you see toys, there may be children; several items in or around a house may point to a certain religion or cultural aspects. Take note but verify later.

You are out to meet a specific person or a specific group of people. Excuse yourself when others start asking for attention. You don't have to explain why; be clear and decisive. Always check whether the people you need to speak to are at or around the house first. If they are not around, others may know where they are. Then, and only then, the "curious" people may just be the ones who can help you out and tell you where you may find them, as they are often well informed. Don't go into detail; just mention it is very important you speak to the resident(s).

The people you want to meet may see you coming. The image of two police officers looking serious and walking up to your house will probably make most people nervous.

Catherine, 64, who lost her brother to suicide

I was sitting on the couch, watching TV, when I saw the police car drive through my street. I didn't get up to watch, because I assumed they were out on patrol. But then they slowed down and stopped in front of my house. They got out and one of them read the name on my letterbox and then looked at his cellphone. The two officers walked to the house and I knew something was wrong. My stomach tightened and I just froze. They rang the doorbell twice and knocked on my window before I could bring myself to get up and open the door to them. Everything that followed is still a blurry memory to me. I just remember hearing his name and "He is dead." I guess I answered questions, but I really don't remember much.

Walking in

There is no way to predict how people will respond. Being clear, decisive, and directive will help you to create privacy to pass on the information you need to deliver. Verify if the person in front of you is indeed the person you need to speak to and keep focus.

If you ask for a place where you can sit down together, most people will automatically walk to a room that is the most comfortable for them in this situation. Follow them. I can't give you a scientific theory explaining this, but it fits Maslow's model: when in distress, people need to feel safe. Familiar places often offer a sense of safety.

Let them sit down first, as they will probably have a favorite seat or chair. If the people you will be informing were working with machines or heat and water (cooking, cleaning, etc.), have them turn things off first.

Sitting down

I always ask where people want me to sit. In an emergency (and I consider this situation to be one), this is not really necessary. But when visiting bereaved people in follow-up situations, I have noticed how they often leave a seat or a chair where the deceased used to sit empty. Especially when visiting people at a later stage after a suicide, make the small effort to ask where people want you to sit. You don't have to explain why; just ask—a small effort. Although it may not be needed in all situations, I have decided to make it part of my routine, and I will ask in every situation, even during a first visit.

The messenger

Please know that the stress response people will experience may limit their cognitive functioning, especially after you have delivered the news. What we see is that an invisible wall will arise between the person speaking the words, delivering the message, and the receiver. It is very subtle, but it is something my colleagues and I have often seen. It makes sense, and I think it is an unconscious coping strategy.

The benefit of going out in tandem is that one police officer can deliver the message and their colleague can step in later, when questions need to be asked and information is needed. Again, I realize that working in tandem is not always possible, so work within your own situation.

Words

The message you are about to deliver is raw. No choice of words is going to make it less tough and rough. Get to the point: "I am so sorry to have to inform/tell you that John is dead/John died." Use these words; don't use other, longer sentences. Be clear, keep it short. And repeat when needed.

Well meant is not always well done. "John went to sleep and did not wake up. He will never wake up again" may pass your tongue with a less raw feeling, but this may be confusing and cause uncertainty. Don't go there. Don't take risks. Be clear.

You may add some details—that's up to you: "John was found with a bullet wound in the head. CPR had no result. He died." But keep it short and clear.

When I am asked to advise police officers on delivering the message, I recommend the shorter version. A brain under major stress will process information in different and cognitively limited ways. Remember that. The damage is already done; a life, a future, a loved one was lost. Your words will have impact, but they need to be delivered.

Information

In some cases, a suicide may be suspected, and you will be able/allowed to inform people about that. In other cases, the cause of death may not be clear at all and will need to be investigated.

You may need to ask next of kin to view and identify their loved one; you may need DNA material or information about their dentist; Or there may be other questions that need to be asked, searches to be done, and evidence collected. These are important aspects in a very complex, difficult, and emotional situation. Focus on the police aspects and stay in an action perspective. This may be extremely hard for the bereaved, but in the end we know, from experience in previous cases, that a thorough investigation will often help people to find answers and closure.

The support phase

After the informational phase, your approach can shift towards a more empathetic one. As you have already read, it is very important to find ways to help those who are bereaved to regain control. This can be done in many ways, by activating people in giving them action perspectives on a physical level (putting the kettle on, etc.) or by finding ways to get into a conversation about the person who died.

It is very important to use the name of the deceased. I always ask people to tell me about them and show me pictures if it feels right to ask. Especially when children are involved, I will look for ways to implement rituals and offer action perspectives; ask them to draw for me, or find a picture and a candle in the house. I can give no one-approach-fits-all advice; simply observe and be creative. Since every situation is different, there are many ways to support people.

When we are working in tandem with police colleagues, this is the part where we come in; police work is wrapped up and we offer support. If you are on your own, delivering the message as a police officer, you are working within a complex dispatch system: some officers will be called to other duties after a very short time; others will be allowed to spend more time with those they have just informed. I have seen huge differences here, and you really need to see what works within your own work circumstances.

In the UK, we have developed evidence-based suicide postvention training. It's called PABBS (**P**ostvention; **A**ssisting those **B**ereaved **B**y **S**uicide) training. But the letters also form an mnemonic: **P**roviding a safe place to talk, **A**cknowledging the challenges the bereaved face, **B**uilding foundations for support, **B**e the person who signposts to help and resources, and **S**ignal hope and understanding. That is what we need to offer in suicide postvention. We will soon start training first responders in a new evidence-based training called ESPR (**E**mergency **S**ervices **P**ostvention **R**esponse) training.

Difficult questions

Why? The most difficult question that may arise after a suicide is the why-question: Why did he/she end her/his life? The only person to answer this question is gone and the question may haunt the bereaved for a long time. You can read more about these complicated feelings in Chapter 5.

We can't possibly completely answer the why-question, even if a note was left or the death was witnessed by others. It's important to validate and reflect the question, though.

Marjory, 33, who lost her husband to suicide

Why, why, why...why did he do this? Why did he leave us this way? I was sobbing and screaming. The police officer pulled up a chair next to me. He just sat there and was silent, while passing on the many tissues I needed. That was so very important to me. He just allowed me to let it all out. After a while, he told me to take a few deep breaths. We talked about what had happened; and he told me that many people had asked him this same question before; and how much sense it made. But he also told me that the possibility of asking the only person who could answer it was taken away when my husband took his life. I am so grateful for the officer's patience.

A ministry of presence. Just being there. Not changing anything, but enduring together. Silence and listening can be powerful instruments. Recognizing that reactions and emotions are completely understandable and normal. Acknowledging the need for answers, but being realistic and honest at the same time. This officer got it.

How? After a sudden death, people may have many questions about what happened and how it happened to their loved one. Depending on the circumstances of the case, we may or may not have information to answer them. Or we may not *yet*, depending on the ongoing investigation. Don't be surprised when questions are very specific; teenagers especially have asked me extremely graphic and detailed questions.

In "the old days," information was often withheld. This was well meant, but we now know how important it is that questions and requests are heard and recognized.

Anne, 64, who lost her son to suicide

I was not allowed to see him and I was not allowed to return home until everything had been cleaned. There was no viewing and he was buried without a chance for me to see him. They told me he had used a gun; and that it looked so horrible that it would be better for me not to ask further questions. Ten years have passed, but I still have nightmares about him. I wake up and I see this image from a horror movie—completely unrealistic, I know. But I can't erase this movie from my mind.

In searching for information, we start to fill in the gaps. Anne's brain turned the word "horrible" into a movie she wakes up to. Indeed, guns and bullets are designed to create horrible damage, and they do. But not to every part of the body. What if Anne's son had been prepared for viewing by covering the damaged part of his body? What if Anne had been allowed to see the rest of him, to hold and stroke the hands she knew so well? Maybe even help care for him, by washing his feet and dressing them in socks and shoes for the last time? What if… We can't turn back time for Anne. But we can listen to her and learn from her story.

Time versus verification: Information management

When I grew up, my uncle was the only person I knew who owned a cellphone. It was about the size of a large shoebox and very heavy. And look at us now; we are all smartphone owners, always online, ready to inform and be informed. News can travel the whole world within seconds, but information management needs to start as soon as a body is found.

A modern reflex we seem to have developed is to grab our phones and share every moment of our lives on social media. When civilians are at the scene of a discovery, many of them will reach for their devices. But this is really an automatic process; my experience is that most people will listen to you when you actively approach them in that moment. Having said that, we live in a free world as far as communication is concerned; we can't tell people what (not) to share.

A body in the park

A jogger was on his circuit of the park when he discovered a body. He found a lady nearby who had her cellphone with her, and emergency services were called. It was a beautiful sunny day, so many people were enjoying the park. When the police arrived, several people got curious and followed the police car to see where it was going. When the police arrived, about 15 people were already near the tree where the body was. Some of them were taking pictures. An ambulance arrived within the next minute. The ambulance crew went straight to the body, but it was clear that the man had died.

The two police officers reported back to their dispatch center and heard that it would take a while for the incident scene investigation team to arrive. They were dealing with a homicide case. The officers were asked to secure the scene.

A realistic situation: two police officers, an ambulance crew, and a curious crowd. In a perfect situation, more officers would come to secure the scene and the investigative team would arrive within minutes. But realistically we know that this will probably not happen. In reality, it is a busy day and the squad is already dealing with a homicide case; colleagues are busy and the officers on the scene will probably also be responsible for informing the next of kin. This actually has benefits; the officers will have first-hand information when questions arise, and the deceased will receive a name, an identity. To these officers, the case will have a beginning and closure.

Now back to the case. We have a scene, now a police scene, a body, and evidence that needs to be protected until it has been processed. In addition, we have two officers, two ambulance staff, and a growing crowd with a view of the body. Since it is a police scene now, the police officers will be in charge; in most countries, protocol requires ambulance staff to stay until a doctor arrives to confirm the death. But ambulance staff will follow police commands. This is a demanding call for everyone involved, not just for the police officers; paramedics are lifesavers. In this situation a life has been lost, a heart has stopped beating, and there is no intervention that can bring the person back.

Action perspectives are important to everyone on the scene; involve your colleagues. In this case, the patrol car may be equipped with some kind of pop-up screen you could set up to limit the view of the scene. Or you could use other items to do so; work with whatever is available. There may be tape that needs to be placed around the scene to mark the area that cannot be entered by civilians from now on. Witnesses need to be questioned. Some people may need support if they are upset by the discovery and the images. These are just a few examples. Use the capacity you have at the scene, and find action perspectives.

The situation poses many challenges to the four people in uniform, not just in terms of managing the scene and the crowd. The clock is ticking; people have taken photographs. Identification needs to take place and next of kin need to be traced and informed.

Imagine recognizing someone you know and love on a social media picture, not knowing what has happened to them. It's not just pictures of a body that can lead to this; sometimes cars and license plates or other belongings are caught on video or photographed and shared online.

Another issue with posting pictures of bodies or body parts is that they can really disturb people who encounter them. As soon as images and videos are posted on open social media, there is no way for us to control or limit the impact on the viewer or receiver.

A third aspect of sharing may lead to later concerns; at this stage, we don't know what happened. This book is about suicide, and in this specific case the death was later registered as one. But sometimes an investigation leads to other conclusions and a death may have been caused (un)intentionally by others; if a case turns out to be a homicide, legal procedures can be complicated by images and videos of the incident scene out on the worldwide web.

Some police colleagues will take a very directive approach while managing the scene; they might close off the area with tape and send people away. My grandfather used to be a chief of police. Back in those days, if a police officer told you to move away, everyone listened and responded as requested. Times have changed, and here we are with a crowd of more than 20 people and two police officers.

I can't give you a fixed plan of what to do in a case like this; you are your own instrument and you have your own ways of approaching a situation. I can only tell you that I have been in many similar situations, and the directive, strict approach did not work for me; people got agitated, some of them even felt entitled to stay where they were ("Hey, I am behind the tape and this is a public area. I can stand wherever I want"). Similar responses may come your way if you demand that people put away their phones. As with any behavioral advice, telling people what *not* to do may lead to the opposite. People need *action perspectives*. Giving them other options of what *can* or *may* be done is much more effective in my experience. If there are only two of you and you have to guard an active police scene, you have enough on your plate, even without an agitated crowd.

So what works for me? I actively approach people:

> Listen, this is a very sad situation. Someone has died and it is important that we find out what happened. If there are people here who saw the deceased before he died, or if you feel you may have helpful information, please let us know. It is important to verify the man's identity, because there are loved ones we will need to inform. I have seen that some of you were taking pictures when we arrived. I want to ask you to keep them to yourselves. This is someone's son, brother, friend—we don't know yet. He could be my son, brother, or friend, or yours. Please help us by not posting his images online. It will take a while for us to confirm his identity and find his next of kin. We want to be able to offer them support when we inform them. As you can see, screens have now been put up and more colleagues will arrive soon to investigate. We would appreciate it if you would just go back to what you were doing and give us some space to work. This is tough on all of us. If any of you feel upset and need to speak to someone, please call the support line/go to the support website.

Whenever I give this example during training or a lecture, I always get cynical responses from my audience: "Yeah, right, like that would work…" But, yes, it often works for me. Most people are overwhelmed by the situation. Their phone is a "safe place" nowadays and they grab onto it. People follow a crowd, but they will just as easily follow you when you actively use (here we go again) psychological alignment. And especially reminding them that this could be anyone's loved one really has an effect.

Again, however, there is no "perfect script" here; I am only telling you what works for me. And sometimes it doesn't; if a crowd is really out to find conflict, you will need to call for back-up. Or you may get lucky and find some help and eustress within the crowd.

A body in the park continued

Two guys in T-shirts stepped forward and discreetly said: "Hi, we are from the fire station around the corner. We are out on a jog. Anything we can do to help?" The police colleague in charge responded and said that the fire service was not needed here. He went back to the scene. I walked up to them and pointed the two men to the fact that it was getting a bit crowded behind the do-not-cross tape. They got what I meant. "Right folks, the screen is up, nothing to see now. Come on, move along and let these people do their work." They moved with them and the crowd dispersed. "Come on, son, put your phone away. And, you heard the lady, don't go posting this online. Imagine the poor guy's mother seeing your picture out there." Two anonymous, sweaty men in T-shirts: to others, they were part of the crowd; to us, they were colleagues offering peer support, happy to lend a hand because that is what we all do best. They hung around until the investigation team arrived and waved as they jogged on.

Too good to be true? Nope, a real example—an action perspective. Work with what you find; use it or lose it. You will often encounter off-duty colleagues and other people trained or experienced in professions or fields that could be useful; a critical incident will bring many people together. A suicide will cause many life lines to cross paths after the deceased ended his or her own life.

Investigating the circumstances of a sudden death takes time, but there is no time to lose in finding and informing next of kin; we don't want them to receive the news through other channels. It's vital that the investigation is done correctly to be able to be as sure as possible when determining the cause of death, but I don't need to explain how important it is to verify the identity of the deceased before going out to find and inform the next of kin. There is absolutely no room for mistakes—just imagine the impact. Sadly, mistakes do happen, but thankfully only in very rare cases.

When next of kin arrive at the scene

When people have gone missing and their loved ones are searching for them, emergency vehicles, especially in small communities, will cause concern and attract attention. People may follow them. Or sometimes a (social) media announcement may trigger next of kin to go to the scene where the body was found. Sometimes they arrive by coincidence. This can lead to very emotional situations—an incident scene needs to stay secured. But a loved one's needs are different; they want to be with the person who died.

Being confronted with the emotional responses of the next of kin is very tough on those responsible for the investigation, but when investigating a police scene, it is important to keep focus. Working in a very technical action perspective helps. Evidence needs to be secured in several ways; the body needs to be examined. You need your rational brain to stay in focus, because your emotional brain would complicate these important tasks.

When a loved one is near, a name may be called in agony and the body you are investigating becomes a person. Your emotional brain is triggered to get itself involved in the case. Because the loved one's needs are so valid, so very understandable, we can identify with them; if this was your son, brother, friend, you would want to be near them. Hold them, hug them, maybe scream and shout at them. This is a hard and often extremely sad situation.

When a body is found outdoors, as in the case in this chapter, the bereaved person is exposed: no building to retreat into, no area you can take them to get them out of view of the curious crowd. Again, you need to work with whatever you have available. In most cases, we have an ambulance on scene. We don't have a patient in there, and the paramedics are always happy to help; ambulance windows are stickered or have frosted glass. Once in there, you are out of view. The walls of the ambulance can provide a closed safe zone.

Think about Maslow's pyramid theory, referred to in Chapter 1; when they are in extreme distress, people drop to the lowest levels of the pyramid and their needs become very basic—according to Maslow, they need safety and a sense of security. Reasoning becomes difficult and often impossible if these basic needs are not met.

The closed back of an ambulance can be a provisional safe place, and within this space a heavy blanket or my own heavy uniform coat can offer an even more visceral sense of security when the whole world is in turmoil for the person you are supporting.

I repeat: there is no one-size-fits-all approach, so remember this is just an example. It can be counterproductive in some cases—for example, with people who respond to the extreme adrenaline rush with agitation and an uncontrollable urge to move. They would become even more agitated if you locked them up in a small space (because that is how it would feel to them).

▓ A body in the park continued

A car arrived on the scene and two people got out. Since an ID was found on the body, we had a name and a match with the picture on it. The people in the car were the parents. After we informed them, the mother broke down in tears. The father groaned, clenched his fists, and marched off. I looked at my colleague and we agreed without words that I would go after the father. My colleague stayed with the mother. The father was taking big steps, breathing very fast. I strode alongside him and we didn't speak for a while. The physical movement seemed to help him deal with the situation. There were no other people on the path he chose, so when the father started to scream and yell, I let him. He stopped and needed to vomit. I told him I was with him. Helped him to take control over his breathing. In my backpack, I always carry baby wipes and water. He freshened up, and I suggested we could walk some more. Before he stopped, I had been walking next to him or a bit behind; I sensed his agitation and I wanted him to take as much space as he needed. After the stop, I intentionally walked beside him but one step ahead. I did not explain it to him, but I gradually slowed down my stride. He followed. His breathing slowed down, and we were able to talk. We spoke about his son and he was able to regain control over his body and his breathing. After a while, we went back to the scene. My colleague and the mother were in the ambulance. It was important to the father to see his son. Since this would also help the police investigation, the police officers took us to the scene. The body was now positioned on a board, covered by a clean sheet, this was lifted and the father confirmed this was his son.

It was important for him to take charge; during our walk, he had felt so embarrassed to have left his wife when she needed him and he felt ashamed about the vomiting. I could explain this to him: the agitation, the physical reactions, the vomiting—normal reactions in a normal person experiencing the most extreme situation a parent can experience. And certainly nothing to be ashamed of.

The officers offered to drive the parents home, but the father insisted on driving himself. We met them at their house and spoke to both of them.

Sometimes cases develop a different timeline than planned. Stay flexible.

Let's assume we are back with our case and the parents did not arrive on the scene. An ID was found on the body, multiple documents/cards stating the same name in his wallet. And the pictures on his ID and on another document clearly resemble the deceased. Later, someone close to him may confirm his identity during a viewing. And let's also assume that the man lived with his parents, in the same house; in this case, you will receive/find information about his next of kin relatively quickly; you have names and an address.

The information you will receive will probably appear on a smartphone, but, if it doesn't, just write it down; make sure you get the spelling right. And make sure you get the first and last name(s) of the deceased. I sometimes ask a colleague how to pronounce a name I am not familiar with. If we both don't know, I will make a mental note to check it with the people concerned later, just as part of a respectful approach. A note on the name of the person who died: he or she may be called by a different name by his/her loved ones.

A big part of our work is about observing and listening; if you hear that people talk about "Mickey" when you are with Michael's next of kin, just wait for a right moment and carefully ask, "I am listening and hearing you speak about Mickey. Shall we talk about him using that name?" or "Would it be OK if we all speak about him that way?" It will be in most situations. And if it isn't, a respectful way of asking will get you an answer to work with.

Honesty

Information management after a suicide is complicated. What can and do you tell? And how do you tell it? The most important aspect is to always be honest, even if the truth is hard to hear and grasp. Work with the information available to you at that moment and with the questions that will arise; see what people need and take it from there.

We are still in the very early stages and people's needs will change. Some people will not yet want, or be able, to talk. Others may immediately experience a need for answers. Be flexible. Some answers will still be under investigation; explain what is happening and when answers might be available. Some answers will be outside your field of knowledge; refer and see if they can be provided by experts who do have them. Some answers may never be found; be honest and realistic. Every case, every situation is different, but here are some of the questions I have encountered:

- How did she do it?

- When did it happen?

- Was he alone or did anyone see him do it?

- How long did it take for him to die?

- Did it hurt?

- Was she conscious when she died?

- When did he die?

- Where is she now and what are they doing to her?

- What did it look like when he was found?

- Did she leave a note?

- Can I see him and take him home?

Just a few examples of what I have been asked. Teenagers have been much more specific, which was quite challenging to me sometimes, as I wasn't really prepared for some of the extremely graphic questions they had. Some of them requested very specific details about what happened to the body, why that was the case, and how it looked. It's important to take them seriously. Informing in an honest but safe way can be a real challenge.

Ellie, 12, who lost her mum to suicide

I was with Ellie (12) after she had found her mom in the bathtub. Mom had died after she had cut both wrists. The bathtub was filled with water, but when Ellie found her mom, it looked as if it was filled with blood. I had witnessed the scene and it looked very disturbing, even to us as first responders.

Ellie's mom had been hospitalized before, after previous suicide attempts. Ellie told me that this, today, was what she had been afraid of these past few years. She was a very bright young girl, and although she was very emotional, she was very aware of what had happened. This was a young girl, who had been taking care of a mom who could not take care of her. It was a very sad situation for this 12-year-old girl with adult-like responsibilities.

As she had only seen her mother's face above the water/blood, she wanted to know how she had died. Since I had that information, I told her that it looked as if she had hurt her own wrists and put them under water. Ellie then said that her mom had tried that before. Why did she die this time?

I explained how the heart is a pump, just like a pump you use around the house. Ellie got that. I then explained that a pump can only function if there is enough fluid to pump around; if a pump runs dry, it will stop working. That happened to her mom's heart; she lost so much blood that there was not enough blood in her body to keep the heart going. And when a heart stops beating, blood flow stops. Oxygen is no longer delivered throughout the body and a person dies.

Ellie was silent for a while and she then said that something else must have happened; there was so much blood in the bathtub. A body could never hold that much blood. Now I had to think for a while and I told Ellie that that was a difficult question. But I could see that it bothered her.

I saw a full pot of coffee, and I asked Ellie to get a salad bowl. I filled the salad bowl with water. I then dropped a few drops of coffee into the water. We watched how the drops dispersed. I put in a bit more and we watched together as this small amount of coffee changed the color of the water in the bowl. I then poured in the rest of the coffee. We watched the water turn dark. And Ellie understood what had happened.

She had many more questions about who was in the house and what they were doing. I asked a police detective to come in and answer a few specific ones.

Ellie's uncle arrived. She had stayed with him before when her mom was unwell, and he immediately offered to come over and pick up Ellie. I gave them some time alone in the kitchen and spoke to the people working at the scene. They agreed to give Ellie and her uncle a moment to view her mom, before her body was taken away for further investigation. It was a very emotional goodbye.

Ellie must be an adult now. I hope life is good for her.

This is not a copy-and-paste script for you. I decided to share this case because it demonstrates that there is no protocol we can use to prepare for these situations; what I did with Ellie may be completely unsuitable for another case, but in this case it really helped her to find answers.

Sometimes we have to think outside the box. She was very smart and wise, and these questions were important to her. So I felt it was important to look for answers together.

Before Ellie left with her uncle, she got to go back to the bathroom, where her mom had been put on a stretcher. The water/blood had been removed, so the image she saw was very different from the one she had encountered when she came home after school. Ellie was allowed to touch and kiss her mom's face. And the detective let her close the cover over the stretcher. She requested and was allowed to help push it to the elevator. Small ways of regaining control.

We left her in her uncle's arms, the bond between them an important anchor to hold onto, during this difficult time.

Listen and hear the questions asked. Answer them in an honest and transparent way. Find words that won't add what doesn't need to be added: no adjectives (horrible, bad, awful, etc.) are needed—the situation is bad enough without them. Only add information when asked for it; in these early stages, it is important to align with the needs of those we are supporting.

CHAPTER 2—SUMMARY

- After a sudden death, next of kin will be informed.

- Sometimes the next of kin will not be the ones closest to the deceased.

- In this digital age, information may get to people faster than we can. We can sometimes prevent this, but it won't always be possible.

- Police colleagues will often be responsible for managing the incident scene and for informing the bereaved.

- Informing next of kin is a very demanding task. You will never get used to it and it will never become easy.

- It helps to prepare and team up as colleagues. There are no strict protocols to follow, but the following steps are important:

  - Verify information so there is no room for mistakes.

  - Don't waste any time, as information can travel fast.

  - Prepare and, whenever possible, team up.

- Don't get distracted; focus on your task.

- Be aware of your body language.

- Be aware of people's privacy.

- Establish contact and find a safe location to break the news.

- Take extra care when children are around.

- Be clear and choose your words carefully.

- Deliver the message and repeat it if necessary.

- Know that every person will respond to the news in a different way; these are all normal reactions of normal people reacting to extreme news.

- If questioning is needed, or if evidence needs to be secured, be clear and explain what needs to be done and why this is necessary.

- If questions are asked, you may not be able to answer all of them; take note and see if you can refer them or answer them at a later stage.

- If you are concerned about a person's mental or physical wellbeing, don't take risks but consult a GP or ambulance staff.

- In many countries, as first-responding police officers, you will go out to inform on your own.

- Look at this task as a two-phased task. The first part of this intervention will need a firm approach; you will need to take control by taking on a clear and decisive attitude and body language. After the news has been delivered and other necessary police tasks have been done, the informational part of your intervention is over. A more supportive and empathetic phase may follow. We call this a ministry of presence.

- Time is of the essence, and police officers will often be called to another incident. But taking some time to help people deal with this horrific news is not only beneficial to them but also helps you as a police officer wrap up a very demanding call.

- If bereaved people arrive on the scene when a body has been found, you will have to be flexible.

- Practice psychological alignment and use whatever is available to assist you to give people support and privacy.

3

The Body After Death

This chapter will give you very specific information about what happens to and within a body after death. You will read about identification and viewing aspects, and about specific interventions that may be needed, such as autopsy, embalming, and incident-scene cleaning. These aspects are not always taught in first-responder training, but they can cause uncertainty and anxiety in the bereaved. By explaining to them what is being done and why this is necessary, we can help mitigate feelings of powerlessness.

To view or not to view?

We often see first responders shielding a body from view. This is well meant, and done to protect loved ones from scenes that responders feel are potentially scary or traumatizing. What I have learned is that this assumption is extremely subjective; what may look scary or disturbing to you may look completely different to me or to a third person. This is especially true when someone you were close to has died. Here's a body that is known and loved; don't assume that damage to this body is always too much to view.

Any and every control surrounding the death has been taken away, because the deceased died alone; the bereaved are left behind with many questions and without a chance to say goodbye. The "police scene" has been taken over by people in various uniforms. As first responders, we want to help—to save. But the reality is that we can't save after suicide. So we try to help the bereaved by taking over what seems to be so very hard. But is this helping them?

I feel it is important to let the bereaved decide whether or not to view the body. My experience is that making this decision is almost always possible if you take some time to inform and explain. Be very clear and specific, take your time, and repeat when necessary; people in distress may need some repetition before they can comprehend what you are saying. Use short sentences and work in psychological alignment.

This chapter will give you some very specific information and answers to questions I had when I started working in this field. I hope it will assist you in finding words and ways to explain aspects you may encounter. Because information will help the bereaved (and ourselves) to get past the "adjective state"; if we leave them with adjectives like "awful," "terrible," "shocking," or "disturbing," we are causing harm.

Some people will not want to hear any details or ask for specific information. That's OK. Respect that. But many people will want to know more; hear, listen, and answer, when possible. Be clear. Be honest.

Anna, 36, who lost her husband to suicide

They told me his body was in a very bad state. That I would get traumatized from seeing it. So I didn't. I had a closed coffin for him. There is no way back now, but I wish I could have seen his broken body just once more. I wake up at night with this horrible image my brain has created. And there's no way to correct that now.

Anatomy of death

People can end their lives in many different ways. Some ways may leave the body intact; some may damage a body very severely. And a body may not be found immediately. The human body is a miraculously designed, built to keep us alive, fight off diseases, and heal itself when hurt. After death, several natural processes will start to deconstruct the body in a natural recycling process, a sort of self-digestion.

Thinking about these things may be scary and disturbing to many, especially when a loved one is involved. I feel that clear, factual information can assist us when needed and requested. Since we may encounter several aspects of the body's deconstruction process, it is important to understand them, so we know what to expect and can prepare for what we will see. And to explain things to others, when this is appropriate. The literature and science describe specific timelines for these processes, but I will keep the information general. Many factors (temperature, humidity, etc.) influence timelines. Let's leave the specifics to the experts in police and medical examination.

The next part will be quite graphic, as I will give you the information I wish I had had when starting this work.

Decomposition

As long as the heart beats, it pumps blood throughout the body. Red blood cells pass the lungs, pick up fuel (oxygen), and deliver it to tissues and organs, picking up waste (carbon dioxide) on their way back to the lungs. When a heart stops beating and a person dies, cells throughout the body are deprived of fuel and begin to accumulate waste. Chemical reactions start to take place—a process called autolysis. The body's internal chemicals and enzymes start to break down tissue and organs.

Skin discoloration (livor mortis)

After death, blood is no longer moved by the pumping heart, so gravity takes over. Blood cells move to the lowest places in the body. This happens within minutes after death, and within the first hour discoloration may be seen: skin may look purple or deep red in parts of the body lowest to the ground. Skin on the upper side of the body may turn very pale (pallor mortis), as gravity moves the blood cells downward. If the skin is compressed in locations where the body touches the ground or objects, these areas may not discolor.

John, 36, who found his colleague

When I found him, he was lying face down, on his stomach. I rolled him over and I was startled by the color of his face; it had large purple spots. His body felt cold and I knew he had died. When his body was taken away after the investigation, hours later, it looked liked the spots had moved. It looked eerie and I am grateful someone explained to me why that had happened.

For several hours, blood cells will move with gravity after a body is moved, as in John's example: he turned the body around and the discoloration he saw changed. Medical examiners use this information when determining the time of death; after a certain amount of time, the discoloration will no longer change (move) when the body's position is changed. It is therefore important that investigators ask whether the body was moved before first responders arrived, as the location of discoloration can give the examiner information about the position and circumstances surrounding the death.

During the first phase after death, spots will react to touch, similar to when you suffer sunburn: if you push the skin, the redness will dissipate for a moment. If there is no effect when the discolored spot is pushed, the examiner will know a person has been dead for a while.

Putrefaction

When we are alive, our digestive system holds a very personal combination of many different bacteria. These play an important role in maintaining our health. When a person dies, the immune system will stop functioning, and bacteria will not be contained inside the bowel. They will start to break down tissue. This is called putrefaction. Since the bacteria are in the lower abdomen, this is where this process starts. Everyone has a unique combination of bacteria; sometimes putrefaction will occur rapidly and be noted immediately; in other cases, the process will develop more slowly.

Visible signs include a greenish discoloration, starting in the lower abdomen. Bacteria produce substances that cause this. They also produce gas and other products causing the smell that is so typical after someone has died. It is a very sharp, foul smell that will stick around for a long time. While the bacteria spread and digest, the gas may cause bloating of the body, which is most visible after a number of days. The gas will push out fluids through body openings during the decomposition process. Fluids may have different colors and consistencies. Just know this can happen. You may hear people working on the incident scene speak about a leaking body. What I have just described may be what they mean. Or they may mean that, at an early stage after death, urine or feces will have left the body; the sphincter muscles no longer contract after death, so bladder and bowel content may leave the body.

Body temperature changes (algor mortis)

After death, body temperature will no longer be managed and a body will start to take on the temperature of its surroundings. Examiners will measure body temperature to get an indication of the time of death, but air temperature at the scene will influence this process. The people doing the investigation have the expertise to interpret this information. For us, it is important to know that we should not influence the temperature at the incident scene before the investigation is undertaken. If a body is in a heated room, the smell may be powerful, and a natural reaction will be to open a window. If it's winter outside, this will have a huge impact on room temperature. Always ask the investigators in charge whether it is OK to open windows or doors.

Another reason to keep windows and doors closed when inside is to avoid attracting insects; flies have a very sensitive system and will find their way to a body. One fly can lay many eggs that will hatch very quickly. Insects and animals will be attracted when a body is outdoors and can damage it before it is found. This will differ in every case and at every location.

Skin sensitivity

You may never encounter it, but if you do, this information will be important: after death, human skin is no longer hydrated and becomes sensitive to touch.

Cody, 56, who lost his son to suicide

Since I could not reach my son, I decided to go over to his apartment to check on him. He lived a few hours away, and weeks of not meeting up often went by. But the fact that he did not answer his phone had me worried. I called his workplace and heard he had not been in that week. When I opened the door, my son's dog came running in a frenzy. The smell in the apartment hit me immediately. I found my son on his bed, the syringe next to him. I was absolutely shocked when I looked at him; the side of his face and parts of his arm were damaged. I really thought that the dog had fed on him and I almost fainted at the thought.

Again, you may never encounter a situation of a death and pets in a home. But if you do, know that what happened here is that the son's dog had licked his face, arms, and hands, as dogs do. In living skin, this is not an issue. After death, however the dog's tongue will damage the skin like sandpaper would. In Cody's case, this information was very important.

Cody continued

The situation felt surreal and like a horror movie; my dead son and his dog preying on him. But then the police detective sat down with me and said that the dog had probably just licked my son, explaining to me how skin changes after death. It did not make a difference to the loss we had to suffer, but I am so glad I could understand what happened. I would never have taken the dog in, caring for an animal that had hurt my son. Now I know he had been doing the contrary; my son's dog has been living with us since. And while we are still struggling to cope, it is comforting to know that he was not completely alone when he took his life. When I hold the dog, I feel close to my son. He is a blessing to my wife and me.

Body rigidity (rigor mortis)

During biology lessons, you probably learned about muscle functioning: muscles contract and relax. The body produces ATP (adenosine triphosphate) to facilitate this process. To produce ATP, the body needs oxygen. After death, this will no longer be available, and a few hours after death the present supplies of ATP will be depleted. In a different process, calcium will be released. This will lead to muscle stiffening in the body. A few hours after death, the eyelids, jaw, and neck will first show rigor mortis and this will spread throughout the body. The muscles will not be able to relax, which will make the body very rigid and keep it in a fixed position. After a few days, cells in the muscles will start to decompose and the rigidity will disappear.

As with other changes in the body, many factors affect the timeline of this process happening. Examiners have the expertise to interpret these signs in a specific case. For us, it is important to know that rigor mortis may be present and a body may stay in a fixed position when it is moved. If the people you are supporting see or have seen this, it may be helpful to explain that this is a natural process that will disappear in time. Muscles are contracted, holding the body in a fixed position.

The look on the face

A myth I want to debunk here is that a person's face can tell you whether there was suffering, pain, or distress when they died. If the bereaved look at a body and conclude how peaceful the person looks, this is a positive experience and I would never change any aspect of it. But often the deceased's facial features may startle people. Depending on how a person died (e.g. by hanging or a bullet wound to the head), the face may look very different to them. It is important not to speak about facial expression in this situation.

After death, the muscles relax and gravity or pressure on the body will be an influence; when rigor mortis sets in, these features will stay fixed for a while. A funeral director can later be of help, but before an investigation or examination is done, no changes to the body should be made. If people are disturbed by what they have seen, it may be helpful to explain physics and gravity, making it clear to them that they did not see any expressed emotion in the face, because that is just not the case after death.

Sounds

Especially when a dead body is moved, sounds may be produced. This happens when air inside the body moves. It is quite normal to hear the sound of a sigh coming from a body while moving it. If there are fluids pushed away by the air, this may produce a gurgling sound. These sounds are not very loud, but when you are in a quiet room, they might startle you. This will probably not happen to us as professionals, but if it does, just talk about it and explain or ask what happened. If new colleagues or other people are around, I prefer to tell people before the body is moved that sounds may possibly be produced. In this way, they are prepared. But it can still startle them when it happens. If it does, just normalize the situation; the sound is normal and can be explained, but it is also absolutely normal to react to it, because this is an extreme situation most people have never faced before; it is absolutely OK to not be OK with it!

Environmental factors

While all the above is happening inside the body, external factors will also influence the body's decay. The decomposition processes will develop very quickly when a body is in or under water. Outside temperature and humidity will be factors. Bacteria, fungi, insects, and animals may or may not be present. Many bacteria need oxygen to survive, so if a body is buried, especially in dense ground, the process will develop much more slowly than when a body is exposed.

While internal bacteria deconstruct the body on the inside, other bacteria will play a role on the outside. Skin will wrinkle and shrink, and change color. Insects or animals may play a role in decomposition, depending on the location of the body and the time that passes before it is found.

Risks and dangers

Myths have existed throughout history, scaring people to keep them away from dead bodies. But a dead body is not "toxic," as is sometimes believed.

Every case is different: a body may be discovered very quickly after death, or time may have passed and decomposition will be in a very advanced state. As first responders, we take precautions during our work. We have to deal with people we have not met before and we don't always know whether they are carrying certain viruses or bacteria. Since a possible risk of contagion is higher if body fluids are present, we wear gloves and (when necessary) protective clothing. After a death, we work in a similar way when touching and handling the body, body parts, tissues, and fluids. Unless there are specific circumstances, normal precautionary measures will suffice.

Smell

When decomposition is very active, the smell surrounding the body may be extremely strong. It is caused by bacteria producing the foul-smelling chemical compounds cadaverine and putrescine while they break down body tissue. This smell may activate a gagging reflex, which is very natural and may occur in almost all of us; our olfactory (smell) system is connected straight to the quick-responding parts of our brain. This is very helpful when we are in danger; if we smell smoke, it is important that we respond immediately. But when working in a situation with a dead body and a strong smell, some of us may very well experience a strong physical response, hindering our work. This may also cause some awkward or uncomfortable situations, when bereaved or other people are around; we need to handle and manage the situation with the utmost respect.

If you experience a physical response while with people, be honest and professional. If you feel it is necessary, just apologize. While feeling uncomfortable, some colleagues will tend to handle the situation using humor or sarcasm. Be aware that this can cause distress; I have seen situations where people had overheard remarks or witnessed behavior that was very inappropriate. Be aware; be professional.

Sometimes it is necessary for investigators to wear masks or filters to be able to work, but this doesn't happen very often.

Some colleagues use tricks to help manage the smell. A very popular trick is rubbing Vicks® under your nose. I am not a fan of that; the Vicks® will actually activate your olfactory system and enhance your sense of smell. Most important, though, you will associate the (to me, very pleasant) smell of Vicks® with the smell of a dead body, and I don't want that to happen, at least not in my brain.

My experience is that the smell will hit you at first, but it will get less strong because your system will adapt after a while. Walk out and get some fresh air when necessary. The smell will stick around for a long time. Shower and wash up. Clean your clothes. In some exceptional cases, clothing will need to be disposed of.

Even after washing and showering, your olfactory system will remind you of the smell. This is normal and it will disappear on its own. If it bothers or worries you; speak to your colleagues. They are probably experiencing the same thing. If a situation was extremely upsetting, the smell may be part of the upsetting aspects you will have to talk and work through, with or without professional help.

The response after a sudden death

I have studied the ways first responders operate after a sudden death in many Western countries. And there are huge differences, even between neighboring countries or states. I could write a whole book explaining them to you. My advice is this: inform yourself about the protocol that applies to your area and field of work. Contact colleagues in other disciplines involved in the response and ask them any questions that may arise.

Go online or contact your local authorities to look into the forms that are used in your region. Find out who will be called and which death certificates are used? Which part of the certificate will be shared with the bereaved and is there a confidential part? How and by whom will that be handled? Print the forms and read them. See if there are difficult words you don't know and inform yourself. When responding and supporting people, they may ask you questions you can anticipate. In general, in every country, when someone has died, we want to investigate and find out:

- Who died?

- How and when did the person die?

A suicide will technically not be called a suicide when it is first reported; it will be handled as a sudden death that needs to be investigated. Each country or state has its own protocol, describing who is allowed to pronounce a person dead. When a suicide (a sudden death) has occurred, the death won't be certified as a death from natural causes. This will only happen if it is clear that an illness or a disease directly caused the person to die. Several countries require the doctor stating this to have been treating the deceased in the weeks before the death.

Now back to the suicide. The deceased will be pronounced dead and protocol will require further investigation. In most countries, the police will be called to investigate the death. In England and Wales, a body will be taken for further examination and a coroner's inquest will follow (specific information is available via a link given in the Resources).

Autopsy

Autopsies are very expensive and in most cases no full autopsy will be needed. As soon as the cause of death is found, most examinations will be finished.

It is very important to explain that when a body is taken for further examination, this is not done in ways we see in movies. People may have very unrealistic ideas about what will be done to their loved one's body, and these can be very upsetting. Explain that medical professionals will be caring for the body, just as they would when working on a living body. This is done in a professional setting, often a clinic or hospital.

Many techniques used to examine living people can also be used when examining a dead person: blood and urine can be tested; X-ray and scanning machines can be used. These non-invasive ways of examining may lead to a conclusion about the cause of death. When this is not the case, or when regulations and protocol demand it, an autopsy may be needed and requested.

A full autopsy is major surgery on the body. It is important we look at it that way when explaining it to the bereaved. The full body and body openings will be examined from the outside first. An incision, most often in the form of a Y, will be made at the front of the body, starting from the clavicles to the sternum and down to the lower belly. The viscera (the internal organs) will be weighed and examined. Brain tissue will be examined and accessed through an incision, most often on the back of the head from ear to ear. If the body is damaged, or other reasons make it necessary, different parts of the body may be opened and examined. After the examination, the body will be closed using staples or sutures. Sometimes certain tissues need to stay with the examiner (e.g. brain tissue). The bereaved will be informed about this.

Whenever possible, I think it is important to inform yourself about the wishes of the bereaved. Do they want the body to be embalmed? Do they want to have a viewing with an open coffin? Do they want to help take care of the body themselves? Are there certain religious or cultural aspects you need to know and may be able to respect? Will the body need to be transferred internationally?

You can ask specific questions at a very early stage while supporting the bereaved. This may just give you the opportunity to respect their wishes.

Anne's wishes

Kate's mother asked me if it would be possible to take care of Kate herself, washing and dressing her for the last time. Kate died suddenly, but the exact cause of death was not clear. She had cut herself and taken several medications. She was a minor, and a full autopsy was ordered after she died. Being a nurse, her mom Anne knew exactly what would follow. It was hard for her to accept that an autopsy was necessary. And it was important for her to be able to take the lead afterwards, taking care of her daughter before the funeral. She did not want the body to be embalmed.

I called the medical examiner and explained Anne's wishes to him. Kate's body was examined at the university hospital. Afterwards, the medical examiner asked several students to come in and work on

Kate's body. It was an opportunity for them to train their suturing skills. Knowing how important this was to the mother, they took extra time and care. Anne rode along when her funeral director went to the hospital to pick up Kate's body. She was involved in every step that followed. She washed the body, dressed it, and did Kate's hair and make-up. Anne later wrote a letter to the medical examiner and the students, expressing her gratitude.

A small effort, but one that was of tremendous importance to Anne.

A contrary situation is when the bereaved decide they do want the body to be embalmed after an autopsy. I will explain later how this is done. It is often done in the USA. The embalmer will need to work inside the body, so it is not necessary to close it before it is transferred for embalming. Medical examiners will appreciate being informed. And I have heard of cases where examiners will prepare small colored sutures in the veins and arteries the embalmer will need to access. A different small effort and a very kind one.

Transportation aspects

Kim, 66, who lost her daughter to suicide

My daughter ended her life while in Kenya. It was hard to receive information. I was relieved to receive a phone call from the Coronor's office and hear that she would be flown home. A first autopsy was done in Kenya, but the British coronor apparently ordered a second autopsy. I did not have to arrange anything and they kept me informed about what was happening. That was very important to my husband and myself.

Yusuf

Yusuf was born in Germany, but his parents were of Turkish descent. It was very important to them to bury him in Turkey. Yusuf died, possibly by suicide, but his death needed to be investigated. An autopsy was requested. I got a phone call from the police, asking me to come over. Yusuf's father was extremely upset, demanding his son's body be given to him. When I arrived, the situation was quite calm, but tense. Suicide is a very complicated issue within the Muslim religion. Being a Christian myself, and knowing how many denominations exist within Islam,

I decided to contact a colleague. He is Muslim himself and came over to support Yusuf's parents with me. He was able to explain and mediate. With a growing number of colleagues, we have an increasing amount of cultural and religious diversity within our teams. In this case, this was of great value. After the autopsy, his father helped wash his body. It was prepared for transport. Yusuf was buried in Turkey.

Transportation of bodies is often done by normal commercial planes; when transportation is needed, religious or cultural aspects will require a certain timeline, involving deadlines between the moment of death and burial rituals. When possible, the first available opportunity will be used. Coffins will be put in the luggage area of regular commercial planes. There are guidelines and regulations that prescribe how a body and a coffin need to be prepared for transportation. You can find them online or contact your local airport or airline. They will have more specific and up-to-date information.

Identification

There are several ways to identify a body. Often a body will be found relatively intact and soon after death. ID papers and cards may be at hand. Attending first responders will compare the picture with the deceased's features. Visual identification may be possible.

In some countries, a bereaved person will, in some situations, need to be taken to see the body of the person who died to make a positive identification. This does not necessarily need to be done by the immediate next of kin, but may be delegated to another person who knew the deceased. If the body was found by a person who knew the deceased, another visual identification will not be required.

When speaking about visual identification, we also speak about viewing. But we also use the word *viewing* when describing the visitation before the funeral, after a body is cared for by the funeral director. Make sure it is clear to people what you mean.

Depending on location, there will be time and space to prepare a visual identification in a respectful way. Hospitals and morgues have special rooms where private viewings can be facilitated. The body may be prepared and damage may be covered. Lighting may be adjusted. Sometimes smell may be a huge factor. In this case, the viewing may take place from behind a window. This may also be necessary when there is a risk of infection or contagion, or when the investigation into the death is not completed and the body may not be touched. Make sure these aspects are discussed with police colleagues before you bring in the bereaved.

Go into the room beforehand and make yourself aware of what the bereaved person will encounter. When doing this for the first time, it helps to do a "senses check": What do you see, hear, smell, perceive? Having to identify a body may possibly be the hardest thing the person you will be supporting will ever be asked to do. We can't do it for them. But we can do it with them.

In preparation, sit down together. Answer questions, describe the steps you are about to take, describe the image they are about to see.

Supporting Jim, 68, after he lost his son, Peter

In a few minutes we will walk down the hallway. We will stop in front of the room where Peter is now. You will decide when you are ready to go in and then open the door yourself. The door to the room is quite heavy. A police colleague and I will be right there with you.

The room is about the same size as this one. But it has no windows and the lights are not as bright. The room was cleaned this morning, which you will probably smell. You will hear the sound of the air conditioning, but the temperature in the room is the same as it is in here.

Peter's body is on a stretcher in the middle of the room. It is partly covered by a green sheet, which we'll leave the way it is. You will not see injuries. You'll see his right arm and his face. His eyes are closed and his skin will probably look very pale to you.

My police colleague will ask you to confirm Peter's identity.

You may decide what happens next. You may walk out, but it's also possible to spend some time in the room. Peter's body will feel a bit cold, should you want to touch him. It's OK to touch his right hand, his face, and his head. But you don't have to.

We need you to identify him now.

We have to be honest and clear, but also build in ways in which Jim can take control of the situation.

If the body is damaged, it may not be possible to identify it by viewing. The body may be damaged during or after the suicide, or decomposition may have set in. If the skin is intact and fingerprints can be found, dactyloscopy can be used. Fingerprints are unique to a person. They may be available in digital systems (passport and/or security files) or taken from items the deceased used.

Another way to identify is to sequence a DNA sample. Investigators will take a toothbrush or other item that contains the deceased's DNA and compare it with a DNA sample from the body. Just as in fingerprint comparison, a DNA match will confirm the deceased's identity.

A final way to identify a person is to request dental records and X-rays from the deceased's dentist. Comparing images and information from the dentist's files with the dental features of the deceased will lead to identification. An X-ray machine may be used.

If any one of the above methods (visual identification, dactyloscopy, DNA, or dental match) leads to a match, the deceased will be identified and no other method will be necessary.

How will we know when a person died?

You have read that decomposition processes can give medical examiners information about the time that has passed since a person died. The doctor or examiner will also look at the eyes of the deceased; pupils will respond for a certain time and the condition of the eye may also help to determine a time of death. Body temperature and room or outside temperature will be measured. Humidity is important to note. Skin changes and discolorations will be noted, and damage to the body registered. Pictures will be taken of the body and body parts, but also of the surrounding circumstances.

Depending on country and region, the examiner will work at the police scene, maybe even finish the case if it can be concluded there, registering a time and cause of death. In many cases, however, the body will be moved for further investigation by the examining doctor or pathologist. An autopsy may or may not follow.

Meanwhile, possible witnesses will be asked to give information. If the body was found by a stranger, they will be asked for information and offered support if they feel distressed by what happened. As crisis interventionists, we have specific flyers to hand out to people so that they can find helplines when they feel they need them.

If the deceased is identified, next of kin will need to be found. The police officers will want to work as quickly as possible to be ahead of (social) media or other people informing them. But, as explained in Chapter 2, haste is not a good idea; it is absolutely vital to verify information. Mistakes and mix-ups must not happen, because they could have devastating effects!

Impact on first responders

Seeing a body after death can be disturbing not only to the bereaved; it may also be scary to first responders. But this is very subjective.

We all go through different life experiences and we bring our own history to our profession. Our senses were developed while growing up, and we each have a unique way of coping with difficult situations. When taking in the image of a dead body, our senses combine what our eyes see, our ears hear, our nose smells, our tongue tastes, and our skin touches. When I studied, more than 20 years ago, I was informed about the situations that would distress me and examples were given: "When body parts are detached, this will cause distress." I now know that this is not correct; nobody is able to predict distress.

I learned that my sensory images are really not leading my judgment when I am confronted with death. To me, my identification with the situation turned out to be a very important one: aspects of the body or surrounding clothing and/or items. They may remind me of people or situations I have encountered in my own life. If images, smells, or circumstances are similar to experiences that were distressing during my own past, a case may be more difficult than others to me. We are all prone to levels of identification. Keep that in mind and seek or offer peer support when you experience or see distress. Don't think you can predict what others will experience; communicate and be open and honest. Work in a team where you feel safe enough to open up; it is OK to not be OK!

Stepping away

I remember this little boy. His daddy had died and my colleague was supporting the mom. I sat down with the little boy and he immediately sought physical closeness, clinging to me like a little monkey. I have worked in close contact with many children, but this case was different; this boy reminded me of my own son. And I felt this little boy came too close. I asked the boy where their bathroom was and walked out. I asked my colleague for a chat and requested he and I changed roles. We did. I went to be with the mother and he went to support the little boy. I spoke openly about this case in our team meeting and later during my own supervision. Being professional means that you know when to set boundaries. I did.

Funeral wishes and decisions

Sometimes a body is released to the bereaved very quickly; sometimes it can take a long time, but eventually the bereaved will need to make funeral arrangements. Until a body is released, the state pays for the care that is needed. After the body is released, the bereaved will most often hire a funeral home to care for their loved one.

There are many cultural, religious, and international differences in funeral traditions and rituals. And we really don't need to know them all. I learn from each case, but I certainly don't know everything. So I ask what people's wishes are and whether are there certain requirements we can respect. Funeral directors are very experienced and don't just know how to care for a body; they are most often amazing with the bereaved, finding out and respecting their wishes.

The next section will have specific and graphic details about after-death care. As first responders, we are not personally involved in these steps. Sometimes when I have responded after suicide, the bereaved were asked to take decisions on what they did or did not want done to the body in my presence. On some occasions (such as when there were regulations and a body needed to be transported), the bereaved were told that certain procedures would follow. I was asked to explain options and procedures to the bereaved, and I really did not have sufficient information to do so when I started this work. This is why I have added the following sections of after-death care and incident-scene cleaning.

Caring for the body

There are huge differences in caring practices between countries and continents. In the US, it is very common to embalm; in European countries, this is done far less often. The UK is not just geographically in between, but it is in practice too: embalming or embalming-light is an option. Sometimes international rules require embalming when a body needs to be transported.

While researching for this book, I came across big differences in funeral traditions. I am well aware that I will be generalizing here, because every case is different and exceptions will, of course, be found.

In general, in the US it is very important to make the body look beautiful after death—as similar as possible to how the person looked during their lifetime. American people feel it is important to view their loved one before and during funeral preparations. Many techniques and different embalming fluids are used to get it just right. When embalmed, a body can be viewed and touched without a cooling device: it will take on room temperature

In Europe, people feel this is too much. Many people actually think that erasing traces of death may even complicate the process of saying goodbye, although it is important to explain to them that signs and damage may be visible. If embalming is done, there is less focus on the lifelike look, and my experience is that less make-up is used. But often there is no treatment of the body at all. A cooling device will be put under the body to slow the decomposition process. Sometimes a viewing is not requested at all; people often tell us they want to remember the person as they knew him or her during their lifetime. In some cases, a viewing will only be open to the next of kin, giving them a chance to say goodbye. Within Europe, there are more differences. In my home country, the Netherlands, for example, it is perfectly normal to keep the body at home and view it there, instead of at the funeral home. In other countries, home viewings are rare. Funerals are often held with a closed coffin.

Given the above differences, and with so many people moving continents, we also see changes and developments in funeral practice. So, again, I just have noticed a difference in general. We do see more cases of embalming or thanatopraxy (embalming-light) in Europe nowadays. In some countries, funerals take place quite some time after death. Embalming is therefore done to preserve the body. Rules and regulations differ. Go online or contact your local authorities to ask about the specific regulations in your region.

Embalming

Embalming is done to slow down the decomposition process in the body. Sometimes this is required to be allowed to transport a body internationally, but most often it is done to facilitate viewing for the bereaved.

Embalming is an invasive procedure, basically a medical procedure done on a human body that is no longer alive. It starts with a washing of the full body. This gives the embalmer the opportunity to assess the state of the body and to decide what will be needed; an embalmer uses many different chemical fluids. Each case will require a specific combination of fluids to achieve the most natural result possible. The embalmer will know how long the body will need to be preserved before the funeral.

An incision will be made, just above the clavicle, where a main artery and a main vein are close to the surface. Two tubes will be inserted: one into the artery and the other one into the vein. A mix of fluids and water will be pumped into the artery by a machine. Arteries and veins will transport the fluids throughout the body. The embalmer will massage body parts to help this process. While fluids are put in, the pressure will push the blood out. This will leave the body through the tube that was inserted into the vein. The blood volume is being replaced by the mixture of water and chemicals. Some of the chemicals are specifically made to influence the color of the skin. But the most important chemical used during embalming is formaldehyde. Formaldehyde binds with proteins inside the body. As explained earlier in this chapter, in a decomposing body cells and tissues are being deconstructed; formaldehyde will bind and keep cells in place, halting the process. Depending on the concentration of formaldehyde used, decomposition will be halted for days or weeks. In the end, however, even embalmed bodies will decompose.

You may have seen bodies of famous people preserved in a mausoleum. These bodies require a huge amount of care and effort and timely replacement of embalming fluids. Mausoleums have teams of embalmers caring for just one body.

If the arteries and veins in the body that is being embalmed are intact, the fluids will reach all parts of the body. But if there is internal or external damage, certain parts of the body may not be filled. The embalmer will access these specific body parts by separate small incisions, entering an artery and a vein to repeat the process and exchange fluids. In cases where body parts are retrieved (e.g. after a railway suicide), it is possible to prepare body parts separately and still have a viewing.

Caring for Dana

Dana's head and torso were severely damaged by the train. She was a sibling in a large family and her parents specifically requested a viewing, so her brothers and sisters could say goodbye to Dana. One arm and the legs were embalmed, and the rest of her body was treated to preserve it by the embalmer. Her body was set into the coffin and the damaged parts were covered by sheets and a quilt that the parents had brought in. The shape of the body under the blanket was set in a very natural way. A large picture was framed and put next to her. Dana's hand and legs were completely undamaged. Her sisters and one of her brothers painted her nails in different bright colors. They were able to touch her, while spending time with her. A bereavement nurse was with them to provide support. A craft table was set up. Dana's brothers and sisters were allowed to draw and paint on the outside of her coffin. Tears and laughter were shared in the room with her, talking about her, remembering the good and bad times they had shared.

When a body is severely damaged, a viewing will not be requested by everyone; many people will not want to see their loved one in this condition. But it is important to inform them about options and possibilities; as long as an informed decision is made, this will be the right decision. Don't assume and conclude for others; involve them and make sure their needs are recognized and met. Saying goodbye to Dana was heartbreaking and extremely sad for her family, but it was not traumatizing for any of them.

After the arteries and veins have been filled with embalming fluids, the incisions are closed. Then, in the next stage of the embalming process, two incisions are made near the belly button. A long instrument (trochar) is inserted. It looks like the instrument used when you see laparoscopic surgery (keyhole surgery) on TV. It has a sharp end and holes near the end. A suction machine is hooked to the end. Remember the description of decomposition I gave you earlier? After death, the bacteria that live in our bowels will start to deconstruct cells and tissue. The embalmer will take out body fluids that hold the many bacteria using this instrument. After this has been done, a separate kind of anti-bacterial embalming fluid is inserted into the abdomen.

After embalming, the body will be closed with great care. Embalmers are taught to use different suture techniques, just like those taught to doctors and other medical professionals.

After treatment, the body is washed, dressed, and made ready for viewing. Make-up and other products can be used to finalize the caring process. Again, depending on where you live and work, embalming may or may not be common. If you don't know, just contact funeral directors in your area and ask them. They will be happy to answer your questions.

Embalming gives the bereaved time to say goodbye, which may be of great importance after a very sudden death. The body will not need to be cooled and will look very natural and familiar. Some people prefer not to recommend it, because they feel the person looks more asleep than dead, which may make the acceptance of the reality of death difficult. Others are against embalming because they believe it is environmentally unnecessary and unethical that chemicals are used after death.

I have given both perspectives here, without any judgment. It is important that you are informed in order to be able to inform those you will be supporting. Whatever they decide, as long as their decisions are based on real and honest information, their decisions need to be respected. It is important that you offer a ministry of presence and psychological alignment, and support them to give informed consent and find ways to take back control.

Embalming after autopsy

At a very early stage, people may be asked whether they want the deceased to be embalmed or not. In the case of an autopsy, it is helpful if the examiner is informed: if embalming is to follow an autopsy, the body will need to be accessible for the embalmer. I explained that the medical examiner will remove the viscera (the internal organs). This means that the arteries and veins connecting them will need to be opened. Embalming cannot be done through one opening after an autopsy. The embalmer will need to use several different entries to different body areas. And since the body has been opened anyway, the embalmer will access arteries and veins from the inside. The viscera will be treated separately, using embalming fluids. Depending on the situation, the viscera will be buried in or with the body.

Thanatopraxy (embalming-light)

In some countries full embalming is not an option, but thanatopraxy may be offered. If thanatopraxy is requested, only the first part—the fluid exchange as described above—will be done. Often, less concentrated fluids will be used, because thanatopraxy will only halt decomposition for days, rather than weeks. This procedure is much less invasive than full embalming. And if a body is kept at home for viewing, in some countries thanatopraxy can even be done at home.

Funeral directors

As with decisions about embalming, the family's decisions about funeral arrangements should be based on honest information. A good funeral director will respect the family's wishes without the sole focus being on making the biggest profit; funerals can become very expensive.

Depending on options available in your country, it will need to be decided whether there will be a burial or a cremation. In some countries, other methods are researched, using extreme cold or substances to deconstruct body tissue. This is a decision that needs to be made with assistance of the funeral director, who can inform about options and costs. If there are religious ceremonies or rituals needed before or during the funeral, others will be involved.

A suicide often happens very unexpectedly and suddenly. Financial reserves may be limited. Decisions on funeral arrangements will have to be made despite the despair and distress.

Did the bereaved and the deceased talk about death and specific wishes? Did the deceased leave written instructions, and is it possible to respect them?

Funeral directors know how to assist the bereaved through the necessary steps. I have seen some amazing professionals, who sometimes even added pro bono services, when money was an issue.

Cleaning the scene

Depending on how the deceased died and when the body was found, (professional) cleaning may be necessary after the investigation is done.

The worst scenario

In countries where guns are available, we see many gun suicides. Depending on which gun was used and how the body was damaged, a lot of cleaning may be needed. In countries like the USA, where many guns are in circulation, there are many cleaning companies that specialize in incident-scene cleaning.

Another reason for professional cleaning may be the state of decomposition in a body; if a body is not found immediately, decomposition will set in. Fluids from the body may get into furniture, floors, and walls. If this happens, it will be necessary to seek professional advice; if natural materials such as wood are affected, it may not be possible to save them. Sometimes floors and walls have to be deconstructed or treated by specialists. Ozone machines may be used to neutralize the smell in a building. Delegate this to specialists and don't take risks.

In many cases, professional cleaning will not be necessary. Even if this is not their responsibility, often the people doing the investigation or the funeral company that has been hired will have cleaned up a scene before you go back to it. But you may be confronted with body fluids or tissue. Some colleagues would advise you to clean up (or arrange to have it cleaned up) so that the bereaved will not be confronted with something that may be traumatizing for them. That is a point to consider. I prefer to go in and have a look myself first. I will then go back to the bereaved and talk to them. Some may request that others clean up and they don't want to go back to the scene before everything is done. But others will insist on cleaning up themselves. This is a way to take back control, and, if people know what to expect, my experience is that this will not be traumatizing for them.

Grace, 45, who lost her son to suicide

My son had died in the bathtub. He had used a knife to end his life. There was a lot of blood. After the investigation they took his body away and most of the blood was gone. But not all of it. My husband didn't go near the bathroom, but I felt this urge to clean the room myself; this was my child, this was his blood. It was the last thing I could do after he left me out of his last decision. So I went and did it. I was crying, screaming, angry, all at once, while scrubbing. But it was what I needed to do. And I am glad I did it.

When Grace told me she insisted on cleaning herself, we prepared together.

Blood will stay fluid at first, but after several hours it will become gel-like before it dries up. If blood has not dried up, pick up as much as you can using paper or cotton disposable towels before adding any fluids; wet cloths or water will just spread it around. If blood has dried, use a paint knife or spatula to remove it. When cleaning, don't use modern spray disinfectants; body fluids contain proteins and organic cells. Use old-fashioned neutral soap instead. Wear gloves and other protective clothing, just as you would when working around body fluids of a living person. If you have more specific questions, ask the funeral director; he or she will be able to answer them.

CHAPTER 3—SUMMARY

- A dead body is a loved one's body to those who loved and lost.

- What may be disturbing to one person will not cause distress in another person.

- It is important that the decision whether or not to view the body is left to the bereaved. You can assist them and give them the information they need to make the decision.

- Sometimes viewing is necessary to identify the body.

- Be sure to prepare and support people before, during, and after viewing.

- Other possible ways to identify are fingerprint recognition, DNA sequencing, or identification by dental record.

- Explain to the bereaved what needs to be done and what is being done to determine the deceased's identity and to answer questions about when, where, and how they died.

- An autopsy may be ordered.

- If this will take some time, inform people even if this complicates cultural or religious timelines and rituals after death. Be clear; be honest.

- A body will be released to the family as soon as the investigation is finished.

- When confronted with a dead body, people will also be confronted with changes after death. Questions may be asked. Answer and explain.

- Skin discoloration will occur, because gravity will cause blood cells to move to the lowest parts of the body.

- Decomposition will start to deconstruct cells and tissue. Chemicals and bacteria inside the body will lead to discoloration and a typical sharp smell.

- The body will take on the temperature of its surroundings and chemical processes inside the muscles will lead to temporary stiffness.

- Being in water or exposed to warm weather will speed up decomposition. Bacteria, insects, or animals may affect the body's state.

- Changes in the body will help a medical examiner to determine the time and location of death.

- Non-invasive examinations such as scans and X-rays may be used to determine the cause of death.

- If an autopsy is needed, the body will be opened and examined.

- In some countries or cases, embalming may be requested. The body will be treated with chemicals to temporarily slow down decomposition and allow viewing.

- If cleaning of the location where the body was found is required, referral to professional services will sometimes be necessary.

4

Communicating After Suicide

This chapter will explain how communication can either increase or lower suicide risk. You will read about the Werther effect and the Papageno effect, and about dos and don'ts in communicating about suicide. I will show you how you can apply guidelines when supporting people after suicide. You will also read about suicide notes and how they can vary.

How to talk about suicide

Suicide takes lives in every culture, and it affects people on every continent—people with every skin color, social status, profession, and gender. It can happen anywhere and affect anyone.

Thinking and talking about it can be very scary, as we would rather not be confronted with this reality and just walk away. Suicide is surrounded by taboos, which you will read about in the next chapter.

How do you talk about suicide? What do you say? Many people don't know which words to choose and avoid the subject. Others will say they have heard or read that speaking or writing about suicide may increase suicide risk for others.

Much research has been done on the subject and I have decided to devote this chapter to communication after suicide, because it is so very important.

It is my hope that everyone involved in the immediate aftermath of a suicide will receive support and training in suicide postvention, but that is currently not the case. This chapter will give first responders a basic knowledge of what is important in communication. Words matter and words can make a difference.

You will find literature links to a handout, media guidelines, and research in the Resources list. I have studied them and will give you an overview. And I will give you some examples from my experience to help you find the right words after a suicide. Make sure you choose and use your own words; don't just copy and paste mine. Educate yourself about the dos and don'ts and implement them in your own way. That will make them real and sincere.

Werther versus Papageno: How communication can influence suicide risk

We're talking literature and opera now! How did that happen?

When suicidologists started to research the effects of communication and (media) coverage on suicide, they found both negative and positive examples.

In the literature you will read about the Werther effect (and how it increases suicide risk) and the Papageno effect (a way of communicating and lowering suicide risk). I will explain how we got to them, because if you are going to use both effects in explaining risk factors, I want you to at least have the following background information.

Afterwards I will give you some communication strategies. You will recognize several aspects from both Goethe's and Mozart's work in the current strategies and guidelines we use. Interestingly enough, both works were published in the second half of the 18th century.

Werther effect

You may have heard of the German author Johann Wolfgang von Goethe. His first book was called *Die Leiden des jungen Werthers*. The title was translated into English as *The Sorrows of Young Werther*. I would have translated the word *Leiden* as *sufferings* instead of sorrows because I feel that would have described the content better.

The book is an epistolary novel, a collection of letters written by Werther, a young man writing about love, art, and the struggles of life.

Werther is in love with a woman who is already engaged to another man. She can't possibly court two men and she distances herself from Werther, who then decides that everyone would be better off if he died. He describes his reasoning, and his suicide is presented as a solution to a problem he can't solve.

Goethe then has Werther describe his suicide plans in detail. He takes the reader through the steps leading up to the moment he uses a gun on himself, and his death many hours later.

The book was published in 1774 and it quickly became an international bestseller. Even Napoleon Bonaparte loved it. Many young European men identified with Werther. He became an idol to some, who dressed the way Werther dressed and took on his lifestyle. His struggles and sufferings were universal to many young people going through situations of love and loss, suffering broken hearts and dreams.

The problem was that they also identified with the solution Werther had chosen; many young readers died by suicide, and some even copied the exact circumstances in the book.

Goethe felt horrible and distanced himself from the book. For about 50 years was banned in several countries, because people were shocked by the number of suicides by those who had read it.

Copycat suicide

The phenomenon of people copying methods and circumstances in their own suicide is often called copycat suicide. I prefer to speak about suggestive factors and circumstances as *triggers*: many young men identified with young Werther; his sufferings became their sufferings. Reading and reasoning with Werther, the letters in the book triggered suicidal thoughts and consequent suicidal behavior in the reader.

Contagion

As I wrote in the Introduction, suicide risk cannot be found in a DNA test, a blood examination, or other physical testing. Even psychological risk assessments and scales do not give us any certainty about who will or will not die by suicide.

I do believe suicide can be contagious, as Werther's example shows. Sadly, we see clusters of suicides in communities, families, and companies. That has not changed during these past centuries. Methods and circumstances are not always the same, but the solution to suffering tends to be copied when a life is ended.

It is very important to be aware of this when responding to suicide; we know that bereaved people face an increased risk of suicide. Although it may be difficult and taboo-laden, it is important to incorporate this knowledge into our postvention; we need to acknowledge contagion risk and offer action perspectives and helplines to those who may need them.

Papageno effect

You will definitely have heard of Wolfgang Amadeus Mozart, the famous Austrian composer. In 1791, one of his most famous works premiered in Vienna: the opera *Die Zauberflöte*—in English, *The Magic Flute*. The opera is a *Singspiel*, which means that some parts are spoken and some parts are sung onstage.

Many books have been written on this work because the storyline contains multiple layers and, according to some, hidden messages. If you are a connoisseur, please excuse me for simplifying the content here.

The opera is basically a fairy tale—about right and wrong, good and evil—into which are woven two love stories. The first is about two extremely successful and self-confident lovers. And then there's another couple: Papageno and Papagena.

Papageno turns out to be a chronically unlucky person; he keeps failing challenges and always has bad luck, in contrast to Tamino, the heroic character in the story.

Papageno is a funny lad, but when he keeps losing and failing, he becomes suicidal onstage. He has met the love of his life, but when he feels he has lost her, he starts planning to end his life. Before he does so, helpers appear onstage and they guide him through his suicidal phase; they tell him to ring his spiritual bells (Andrea's translation: they help him to regain control and offer him an action perspective). He finds hope and perspective and moves on. In the story, he is reunited with Papagena and they sing a duet about how they will live happily ever after.

Best practice

Mozart shows us how suicide prevention and intervention can be done; a suicidal Papageno, probably in the state of constriction, is only experiencing his suffering and views suicide as a solution to end his pain. He can't look beyond his mental birdcage that causes him to experience tunnel vision and feelings of hopelessness.

And then helpers appear; they remind him that he is not alone, that there is hope. They point Papageno to the tools and the power he possesses, which he had lost sight of. They offer him an action perspective and motivate him to take up their advice.

The storyline shows how Papageno recovers and even regains joy and happiness. This is simplified and maybe too good to be true, but it happens for Papageno. Nowadays, we tend to speak about best practice, showing us how things should be done. Mozart got it.

So there you have it—the Werther effect, used when describing factors that enhance suicide risk, and the Papageno effect, used when describing factors that lower suicide risk.

International guidelines for reporting on suicide

When communicating after a suicide, it is very helpful to keep the international guidelines for reporting on suicide in mind.

You may need to have one-on-one conversations, inform a group of people, or maybe even talk to media, depending on the situation.

Whether you are responding to a suicide in a home setting or need to inform an international audience after a celebrity suicide, the guidelines will always help you to communicate in a safe way. The list below is published by the World Health Organization (link in Resources list).[1]

Responsible reporting after suicide
Dos

- Do provide accurate information about where to seek help.

- Do educate the public about the facts of suicide and suicide prevention without spreading myths.

- Do report stories of how to cope with life stressors or suicidal thoughts, and how to get help.

- Do apply particular caution when reporting celebrity suicides.

- Do apply caution when interviewing bereaved family or friends.

---

1   Reprinted from *Preventing suicide: a resource for media professionals – update 2017*, The World Health Organization, Copyright 2019. Accessed on 3/11/2019 at www.who.int/mental_health/suicide-prevention/resource_booklet_2017/en/

- Do recognize that media professionals themselves may be affected by stories about suicide.

Don'ts

- Don't place stories about suicide prominently and don't unduly repeat such stories.

- Don't use language which sensationalizes or normalizes suicide, or presents it as a constructive solution to problems.

- Don't explicitly describe the method used.

- Don't provide details about the site/location.

- Don't use sensational headlines.

- Don't use photographs, video footage, or social media links.

Much research has been done since Goethe and Mozart lived, but as you can see, centuries later, you can still track these dos and don'ts back to their original storylines!

How to communicate responsibly about suicide
Lost for words after suicide

Bob, 58, who lost one of his senior staff members

I was still hoping I would wake up from a bad dream; one of my managers had ended his life. It happened at the weekend. On Sunday night I went to my office to write a memo to inform all of our employees. I had been staring at a blank Word document, but I did not know where or how to start. We are a people-focused company; personal relationships with our staff and their wellbeing are so very important, or at least I thought so. Now one of my senior managers had killed himself! I had spoken to his wife, who seemed just as shocked as I was. I felt angry, sad, numb... all at once. I couldn't sort my thoughts. Then my phone rang. It was a business contact. The situation was so bizarre already that I didn't think it was strange he was calling on a Sunday night, even though we hadn't done business for quite a while. "Hi, Bob, listen, we haven't spoken for a long time and I will keep it short. We need to catch up, but for now I want to tell you that I heard what happened. And I am so sorry for your loss. Last year my office manager died by suicide. Awful story and we were all a mess. It took me a while to find the right person to help me sort things. I can't help you. But if you are feeling as I did back then, you may want to call the person who helped me. She works highly confidential, trust me. I will text you her name and phone number. Now I will leave you alone. Hang in there, man, you can do this."

He had hung up before I could say anything and I was flabbergasted; we had always been friendly to each other, but there had never been any personal relationship.

My phone buzzed and his message arrived. I stared at it and stared back at my blank screen. I decided to make a phone call.

Bob rang me very late on a Sunday night after receiving my number from someone I had helped a year earlier. He sounded very nervous and was breathing fast—normal reactions of a normal person to an extreme situation.

In a normal situation, a high-profile business manager would probably have checked my background and references, and have had someone do a digital check on me before calling in such a vulnerable and personal situation.

Acute stress has a huge impact on us. This is why I don't think suicide postvention should be done and offered from a business perspective, by people looking for the biggest gain; people are in a very vulnerable state. It is easy to take advantage of that situation.

Suicide postvention (along with prevention strategies) should be implemented in every employer assistant program (EAP)—even for us as first responders and medical staff, not just in commercial businesses. I would recommend that employers don't wait to consider this until a suicide has occurred; you need to plan ahead. These programs need to be well prepared and a normal part of any employer's organization, just like safety and evacuation plans. This doesn't mean employers can't call someone like me to assist when it happens. Just make sure you plan and think ahead and involve competent people who are experienced and trained to provide services. Or get some of us to provide in-company training to set up your own crisis intervention team.

You'll find a link to our UK corporate crisis consultancy website in the resource list. Ask your employer about EAP services and emergency plans. Are they prepared?

Bob continued

So there I was, in the middle of the night, talking to a complete stranger. Heck, I even cried and screamed. And she somehow did not find that strange. I don't remember what we discussed at the beginning of the conversation. She just listened and asked a few short questions, in-between my incoherent babbling. At first, I was stampeding through my office, but somehow I sat down after a while. And I seemed to feel better, or at least my brain felt better, because I found myself thinking again. I told her about Jeff, about our company and about the blank screen on my computer. She suggested I use it to write down my action plan for the next 24 hours.

We discussed options and we agreed that she would come over the next day to plan the rest and to help my EAP staff organize support for our employees.

We then discussed what had to be done before then; I felt I needed to write a memo for our staff, and I wanted to write a notice to inform our customers and business contacts.

I told her how difficult it was to find words. She then asked me a question I still remember, because it really helped: "If Jeff had died in a car accident, what would you have written?" And she promised to mail me a short list of dos and don'ts for writing after suicide. We ended the call. I took a deep breath. I had a plan, and important work to do.

Bob did not even tell me his last name, but he just started to talk when I picked up the phone. I felt that there was a lot he needed to get off his chest, so I adapted to what I felt was needed; I started by just listening, not only to his words, but also to the way they were said. I retreated to a quiet room with a cup of tea and prepared myself for a longer conversation.

These first calls can be one of two kinds. Some people can't find words and are very quiet, and it will take me a while to find a way to achieve psychological alignment. Trust needs to be established and I have to build a conversation carefully.

Or I get calls from people like Bob, during which words seem to form a waterfall, coming from my phone. You could call this *catharsis* (a word Aristotle introduced), which literally means *purification*. In lay language, we all know how it can help if we get some things off our chest—like a bottle of fizzy drink: if you take the lid off, the pressure can get out.

Bob released his emotions. They were blocking his ability to think. He wanted to take control of his situation, but that was difficult.

After a while, as our conversation progressed, his breathing slowed down and I could sense he was becoming calmer.

In Bob's case, the fact that Jeff had died by suicide was a mind-blocker for him; it took up his sole focus. He was angry and sad, and expressed severe feelings of guilt, because he felt he should have prevented Jeff's suicide. (You can read more about guilt in the next chapter.) I acknowledged Bob's feelings and reflected on them.

Imagine holding a mirror. All these complex feelings are like rays, flying through space, and hitting the mirror in chaotic and unorganized ways. By working in psychological alignment, you keep moving your mirror until the rays seem to come together.

Then you can bundle them and the other person gets to understand what he sees in the mirror in a better way; I reflected Bob's thoughts and feelings back to him. I did not add anything to them, I just helped him to organize them. Powerlessness and hopelessness versus an action perspective and control. When Bob experienced this, he could sit down. We made a plan, and he slowly took back control over the situation.

But the mind-blocking effect of the suicide was still present. I asked him to tell me about Jeff. And we spoke about their company and their relationship. An important ice-breaking sentence in this case was a question I often ask: "I am so sorry I never got to meet Jeff. I can see how important he is to you. I would love to hear about him, would you tell me some more? What kind of person was he?"

This shifts the focus from the act of ending their life by suicide to the person himself; shifting attention from their death to the life of the deceased. And it can be very powerful.

After Bob and I had discussed what was needed in his situation, he asked me for further support in assisting his EAP team. They were only recently trained to provide first aid and emergency support, but they had not been trained in psychological first aid. Suicide was a new subject to them. We agreed I would meet them the next day.

Meanwhile, Bob wanted to communicate to both his staff and to his customers in a written statement. The suicide mind-block occupied his empty Word document, so I decided to ask him to change his perspective: If Jeff had died suddenly from another cause, what would Bob have written?

He was silent for the first time during our conversation. And he understood what I meant. I advised him on safe writing after suicide and sent him some brief information. We ended the conversation with a clear timeline and plan.

Before the memo was sent to the staff and the communication for the customers was placed on the website, I read it to make sure it was safe for everyone. I did not have to advise on any changes; Bob had done an amazing job.

Challenges

Sometimes situations pose very complicated communication challenges after suicide; people may have been suffering from mental illness for a while, relationships may have been under huge pressures, or connections may have been lost. Sometimes a colleague may die after being absent, having been unable to work in the period before they died. Or there may have been conflicts and problems between them and others.

Some people seem to want to make a statement by performing the suicide within a public location or their work setting. Or they may leave a note or message, accusing others of causing their suffering and consequent suicide.

Although this is rare, we do see cases where methods and/or messages contain a huge amount of aggression and anger towards others.

This is an incredibly difficult situation which can cause huge amounts of distress to people and damage to relationships within families, communities, and companies. We can't prevent the primary damage caused by suicide; life is lost before we are called. Suicide postvention can prevent secondary damage when we create a situation where people can feel supported and heard; where honest words can be spoken and feelings, both positive and negative, may be shown and shared.

When we respond within corporate settings, offering crisis consultancy, employers will talk about business continuity and the monetary benefits of our service. And, indeed, suicide postvention hugely assists in mitigating the impact of suicide on a business; suicide has the capacity to destabilize the most successful organizations and teams. When evaluating our work, we hear that teams and employers have experienced how important suicide postvention has been, both from a personal and from a business continuity perspective. We also like to talk about what we call human continuity, while helping people to help themselves and offering a compassionate presence.

Conflict

Harriet, when conflict arises

Harriet had been put under investigation by her company's management, because there were doubts about financial transactions that she had handled. This had been extremely difficult for Harriet. She had just ended a relationship and was in major debt. The investigation caused tremendous amounts of shame and anger, and it had been hard for her to cope. After she died by suicide, her parents found a note. Harriet had written in a very angry way and accused her employer of giving her no other choice than to end her life because she felt the investigation had ended hers. The note was clearly written in a state of despair and some parts of it were very incoherent. Her parents had not known about the investigation and were shocked to read how it had affected Harriet. A huge amount of anger and rage developed.

This is a situation that is really not uncommon. Unfortunately, we see devastating effects if it is not handled with care and support. Again, postvention can't do or offer anything to change the primary damage present: the loss of life. However, secondary damage may be prevented—sadly not always, but it is important we try.

Harriet continued

Harriet's employer had ordered his EAP team to organize a short memorial meeting two days after Harriet had died; employees were invited to gather and remember her. Her parents were informed that this would be done. They received a copy of the leaflet handed out to staff, and they were asked if it would be OK if the fact that Harriet had died by suicide could be shared, so other staff could receive more specific support. The parents had agreed to this immediately after the suicide, but in the days following, their levels of anger and frustration had risen. When the short memorial meeting started, Harriet's mother walked into the conference room. She was very emotional and angry, and she made accusations, blaming the company's management for her daughter's death. She then left.

This was a devastating situation; EAP staff had carefully prepared their meeting. Now they had to deal with a completely unexpected situation, as only a few people in management knew about the investigation; many people in the room did not understand what had just happened. Harriet's parents were devastated, of course, but in a different way.

A very difficult period followed. Groups of colleagues got in touch with Harriet's parents, feeling that they had to find some kind of justice for Harriet. Others formed groups supporting the colleagues working to investigate missing funds and integrity issues.

The company recovered, but it took a long time and many hours of professional and legal mediation to find peace.

Several employees left the company. Mediation was offered to bring management staff and Harriet's parents together, but sadly this did not lead to closure for them. Harriet's mother is still seeing a therapist and struggling with the situation.

Could things have been done differently and complications prevented by offering specialist suicide postvention in a very early stage in this case? We will never know. But after learning from cases with a lot of secondary damage, like the one above, we are investing in improved communication at a very early stage after death.

Communication is so very important. And sometimes, despite well-meant efforts, problems arise. Suicide is complicated. Its effects can be devastating in so many ways. Nobody will ever be able to write a protocol covering everything that will be needed after a suicide, because we are working with people—people with their own coping strategies, histories, and relationships, and their experiences, positive and negative.

Finding honest words

I have just described a positive and a negative example of what may happen after suicide, but there is so much in-between.

When asking people to tell me about the person that was lost, many different answers will follow. Nobody is perfect; we are all imperfect human beings. And we live our lives in our own unique ways— sometimes in conflict, but often in harmony.

Something I didn't find in the literature, but which often can become an issue after a suicide, is that people sometimes feel they have to avoid negativity and criticism when talking about the person they lost. Since suicide is such a difficult subject to discuss, I often find that people seem to want to overcompensate in positive terms when speaking about the deceased. They often feel sorry for the one who died.

Don't get me wrong, I think it is beautiful to honor the person with a beautiful and respectful memorial. But words should be honest and real and chosen carefully, because taking on an overly positive perspective can cause conflict and tension, which is something I have often seen happening within families and companies. It may become clear what I mean if I give you an example.

Bridget, 25, who lost her uncle to suicide

Uncle Frank had been picked up by the police twice in the weeks before he died, once for domestic abuse and the second time for driving under the influence of drugs and alcohol. Aunt Sally did not want to press charges against him, so he was not arrested. Her arm was still in a cast from the abuse when Uncle Frank was buried after his suicide. Uncle Sam spoke at the funeral. He lives far away and we hadn't seen him for years. We were all attending the funeral with so many mixed emotions; we were grieving the loss of someone we loved and lost, but his death was also somehow a relief. I felt bad for thinking about it that way, but it was; the abuse had ended. Uncle Frank had refused any help and his use of drugs and alcohol had caused so much harm. Uncle Sam spoke about his brother in the most fabulous way. If you had listened and not known him, you would have thought Uncle Frank had lived the life of a saint. It made us all very uncomfortable; Aunt Sally just sat there. She later told me that she felt invisible during the eulogy. I know Uncle Sam meant well. It just didn't feel right to us.

Uncle Frank's family was supported by one of the priests I have trained. He had been called to the family before, after the abuse had happened. When he was informed about the suicide, he immediately went over to their house. Uncle Sam had flown in on a last-minute flight and the priest had not had any time or opportunity to help him prepare his eulogy.

Bridget continued—Father George

I could sense that the eulogy of the brother of the deceased wasn't received in a positive way by his family; they were clearly trying to not show this, but many of us felt very uncomfortable. The brother spoke very highly of Frank and he did not mention any difficulties or the fact that he had died by suicide. This is something I would also never share without permission from the bereaved. However, in this case they had specifically requested me to be open and transparent, because the complicated family situation was not a secret to the people attending the funeral. I wanted to respect the brother and his efforts, but I also wanted to respect the needs and wishes of the other family members. In my sermon I picked up some aspects from the brother's eulogy, acknowledging Frank's life and achievements. But I also added the difficult situations he had encountered—his unemployment and the loss of one of his children, the difficult period that followed when Frank tried to find comfort in substance use, and how it became abuse. I mentioned the many loving efforts his wife and children had made to find ways to help Frank, and the sadness we all felt when Frank would not accept any form of support, ending in his tragic suicide. I decided to add an extra intercession to my planned intercessory prayers. I had already written some sentences on suicide, praying for help and support to those in need, because hope must never be lost, even in the midst of despair. I added: "Merciful Father, please help us all to get through this difficult time. We feel sadness, we have so many questions. To Frank, but also to You. We are upset, yes even angry at times. Please guide us through all these complicated feelings."

I later sat down with Frank's brother. He thanked me for my words. The whole family became closer after the funeral. Sally and Sam speak once a week now. They are healing together.

Never underestimate the power of words. They can break, but they can certainly also bind and bond.

I hope and pray that all religious institutions and seminaries will add suicide prevention, intervention, and postvention as subjects in their curricula. Father George and many others are making a difference.

Now back to the subject of over-positivity. Make sure you listen very well to what is said both verbally and non-verbally by family members, friends, and colleagues.

Mediate and mitigate when you feel this may be needed.

Corporate postvention

I was having a closed meeting with six of Tom's closest colleagues. I asked them to tell me about him. I could feel there was a lot of tension in the room. Every time someone tended towards something negative about Tom, someone else would correct and change the subject to something positive. I then intervened and explained that it is perfectly normal to experience all kinds of thoughts and emotions after a suicide, and they certainly are not always positive, because distress and anger are just as normal as sadness and grief. One of Tom's colleagues immediately burst out, "Then let me be the first to say that I am pissed off with him. How can he leave his wife with two young children? I trusted him with some personal stuff and he always told me to never give up. And what does he do? He just gave up! I am so bloody angry with him!"

Everyone took some deep breaths, because that statement really cleared the air in the group. Others opened up and we had a very important meeting, because important words were allowed to be spoken.

Allowing people to vent all kinds of emotions is very important. Make sure this is done in a safe and confidential setting. If you have been bereaved by suicide yourself, you know how complicated all of these feelings can get; if we are only allowed to discuss the loss and grief from a positive perspective, other feelings may get stuffed away and cause tension. Anger and even relief are acceptable feelings after suicide. Experiencing and voicing them to others in a similar situation can really help. This is why peer support groups can be so very beneficial to people.

Opening up about negative emotions doesn't make you love the person you lost any less. Tom's team organized a beautiful memorial honoring his life. And they raised funds to set up scholarships for his children. When a new conference room was built, it was named after Tom.

Now back to the guidelines. They are set up for people reporting on suicide in the media (written, spoken, and online). But they also provide safe information in other cases when providing suicide postvention. You can use the WHO guidelines or find similar ones online or you can mold them into your own. Whatever works for you, as long as you use the scientific basis to build on, that is fine (links to the science background are included WHO download). I'll write further on the WHO guidelines because they can be applied in every country, on every continent.

Dos and don'ts when reporting after a suicide
Dos
Do provide accurate information about where to seek help

In working with the aftermath of suicide, it is important to be informed about your own national/federal suicide prevention network. When you advise people on communication after suicide, you will be advising them always to add a suicide prevention helpline to any communication.

Don't provide a complete list but inform yourself about services that are known and of high quality. Make sure you provide correct contact information and availability.

If you want to provide resources or handouts, make sure they incorporate accurate, up-to-date information and contact data. And see if you can add bereavement support links for your region.

Do educate the public about the facts of suicide and suicide prevention without spreading myths

Make sure you inform yourself about myths and facts (see Introduction) and stick with the facts. If rumors make the rounds, answer them with facts and verified information.

The key message we want vulnerable people to hear is to never give up hope; help is available and healing is possible. We want them to give them information to find quick access to support.

Do report stories of how to cope with life stressors or suicidal thoughts, and how to get help

This guideline was added to motivate us all to share stories of hope and healing; it features people who were suicidal but who found help and recovered. If you incorporate the aspects that were helpful to them into your story, you are providing a positive example. Do it like Mozart!

Do apply particular caution when reporting celebrity suicides

If a cause of death is still being researched, there will be much speculation on (social) media. Don't share rumors. If the suicide is confirmed, don't glamorize it, as we know this may lead to other suicides following the celebrity's example.

Instead, report about their life, and don't hesitate to show the negative impact of the loss by suicide. Always provide suicide prevention helplines in every communication or in on-screen ticker tape.

Do apply caution when interviewing bereaved family or friends

In Germany, we are very reluctant to show bereaved people in the media at an early stage. I know people in other countries have different perspectives.

When in crisis and under acute stress, it is often better to postpone important decisions, if possible. Whether or not one should appear in the media is a big decision. Because, nowadays, once online means always online.

People bereaved by suicide are vulnerable and at an increased risk of suicide themselves.

The reason why we are reluctant is not just based on the decision-making argument; sometimes journalists will have details or information not yet known to the bereaved. If these details are shared without professional support, they may cause secondary damage.

Later on, when the first phase is over, appearing in the media may be a beneficial to some bereaved; sharing their story to help raise suicide awareness can be very powerful. If the reporting is done in a safe and professional way, the bereaved can really make a difference and help prevent further suicides.

Do recognize that media professionals themselves may be affected by stories about suicide

This is a subject close to my heart because I get to work with journalists in several settings, offering them after-incident support. Journalists just don't get enough support to handle all the news they have to digest. Suicide is a very difficult subject to cover. If you are in contact with journalists after a suicide, advising them or sharing information with them, take the opportunity to add an offer of support. I will say something like "Hey, listen, we don't just support the first responders and the bereaved, we are here for you too. Here's my card if you need a confidential ear. Because this is a tough case. On all of us".

Don'ts
Don't place stories about suicide prominently and don't unduly repeat such stories

When celebrities die by suicide or when a suicide has occurred and has been witnessed by many people, media will be reporting. Experts advise newspapers not to place these stories on front pages; instead, they should be put on an inside page, and towards the bottom of a page. In other words, don't place them in a prominent position. The same advice is given to TV shows and websites: don't cover the suicide as the first or main item. And prevent frequent updates or repetition of the information. More subtle coverage has shown to lead to less subsequent suicidal behavior.

Don't use language which sensationalizes or normalizes suicide, or presents it as a constructive solution to problems

Avoid words that add to what happened: "killed himself," "self-murder," and "committed suicide" come with a negative connotation. Suicide is not a crime. Instead, say "died by suicide," "took his own life," or "ended his life." These are more neutral descriptions.

Avoid using "copycat suicide" or "suicide epidemic." These sensationalize what happened. Instead, refer to "an increase in suicide."

Don't describe the causes of the suicide, because this often leads to the suicide being presented as a solution to suffering. This should be avoided.

Don't explicitly describe the method used

In specifying the method used, you may trigger vulnerable people to copy what happened.

People with suicidal thoughts have told me that specific descriptions give them an image that is very powerful in attracting their attention. These descriptions may sometimes even cause a longing to create a similar situation as a solution to end their own suffering.

If a suicide method used is very spectacular or new, it is important to inform journalists about this risk, as they will often want to report this novelty. This can lead to suicide contagion, as we have seen in the past. Use caution.

Don't provide details about the site/location

You may know sites in your region where multiple suicides have occurred—bridges, buildings, railway crossings, or other locations. Don't promote those locations as "hotspots" or "suicide sites." Vulnerable people may be drawn to those locations if you do.

Don't use sensational headlines

Headlines draw our attention. Make sure you don't include the word "suicide" or any of the aspects mentioned above (method, location) in your headline. This will draw unnecessary attention and increase risk.

Don't use photographs, video footage, or social media links

Photos or videos may hold clues about the suicide method and/or location, and should therefore be avoided.

If you want to use photographs of the deceased, privacy must be respected. Make sure the bereaved give you permission to use materials.

Don't publish suicide notes, emails, messages, and social media posts from the deceased. If you feel some posts could be important in educating about suicide prevention, seek advice from an expert.

A last written communication: Suicide notes

Some people leave suicide notes, and some don't. Before our digital age, Professor Edwin Shneidman wrote an excellent book after studying thousands of suicide notes (see Resources). Just like suicide itself, the subject of suicide notes is complicated. Nowadays, we see other last messages sent through WhatsApp, email, or other channels. I have also seen messages written on mirrors or communicated in other ways.

It is important to know that a note or a message will be viewed as evidence in the investigation, into the death. So it is important we handle it that way. Make sure this is explained well to the bereaved; a note will need to be investigated, but it will always be handled with great care and returned if the bereaved wish to receive it afterwards.

Suicide notes vary enormously. Some are written with a tremendous amount of love and care and can become very important to the bereaved in the healing process. Others are written in a completely different tone, sometimes even very aggressive and angry towards the people receiving them. Some are very short; others consist of many pages.

Some are very well written, their preparation probably starting long before the suicide; others are incoherent, clearly not written in a healthy mental state.

Looking at a suicide note while responding after suicide always gives me a strange feeling; someone has died and yet they are communicating to you. Being confronted with a suicide note feels eerily responsible; here's the last message of a person who meant the world to others. He or she held that note, and I always feel sad when I realize how alone this person must have felt while writing it.

On the other hand, we are looking at evidence in a case under investigation, so that is also something I need to consider; it is vital to be professional. Although it doesn't happen often, notes may turn out to have been written by another person if the case turns into a homicide investigation.

When I see a suicide note, I am also looking at something that may be of tremendous value to the bereaved. But I have to explain to them that we must leave it untouched, just as we have to leave the body to be investigated. This can be very hard on the bereaved; this is their person, their body. And this is their note, they often feel.

Suicide notes and suicide messages come in many variations. I will give you a few examples of cases.

Karen's brother

Karen's brother had damaged many of his personal possessions before he died by suicide in a very aggressive way. He left a note blaming his relatives for his situation and his consequent death. Karen was very sad, but not surprised, when we informed her about her brother's death; he had threatened to end his life during situations of conflict before. Karen told us she had taken the very difficult decision to distance herself from her brother a few weeks before. The police colleague explained that a note had been found and that the content was very negative. Karen immediately said that she did not want to see the note or hear about its exact content. The note was filed, so it would stay available if Karen changed her mind later.

Emile

Emile did not turn up at his workplace on a Tuesday morning. His colleagues found that strange, but they assumed he had got caught in traffic, which was extremely busy that day. At 9 am exactly, 20 colleagues all received a similar email, sent by Emile, using delayed delivery. It was a suicide message, written by Emile. He had arrived in the country as a refugee. There was no family his colleagues could call, so they called the police. When the police went to check, they found Emile's body. He had probably died the evening before, by suicide. The police requested a copy of the email. Support was offered to the recipients of the email through the employer's EAP program.

Noah

Noah died after a fall from a high-rise building. People had witnessed him jumping; he was the only person on the roof. In his apartment, officers found a huge number of notes, put in a box, with the words "To mom, I am sorry, I love you." Noah was suffering psychotic episodes. After the investigation, the notes were handed to his mother. She could not make sense of what Noah had written because they were written in unknown signs and even a police expert had not been able to understand them. Noah's psychiatrist agreed to meet Noah's mother to look at the notes. He could not explain them but Noah's mother was able to find answers to other questions she had. Noah's box received a special place in her house, next to a picture and a candle she has burning to remember him by.

Mary

Mary had been diagnosed with early-stage dementia. When she was found dead, there were packages beside her bed labeled with the names of her husband and her children. She had written very personal documents to each of them. The letters contained explanations and apologies for difficult situations and conflicts she had had with each of her family members in the months leading up to her death. She had put in personal artwork and personal details. The police were able to get permission from the state attorney to investigate the documents at the scene. This way, the letters could be handed over to Mary's loved ones immediately and did not have to be taken and held. Mary's death had a tremendous impact on all the first responders that attended the scene. We got permission to sit them all together at the end of their shift and talk about what happened before everyone went home.

CHAPTER 4—SUMMARY

- People bereaved by or confronted with suicide are at an increased risk of dying by suicide themselves. Communication can either increase or lower this risk.

- The Werther effect describes a way of communicating that increases suicide risk. Suicide contagion and copycat suicides may follow. This could happen if:

- stories about suicide are reported prominently and unduly repeated

- language is used which sensationalizes or normalizes suicide, or presents it as a constructive solution to problems

- we explicitly describe the method used

- we provide details about the site/location

- we use sensational headlines

- we use photographs, video footage or social media links.

⦿ Instead, we should make use of the so-called Papageno effect. If we use communication in a different way, we can lower suicide risk and help prevent further suicide. This could happen if:

- we provide accurate information about where to seek help

- we educate the public about the facts of suicide and suicide prevention without spreading myths

- we report stories of how to cope with life stressors or suicidal thoughts, and how to get help

- we apply caution when reporting celebrity suicides

- we apply caution when interviewing bereaved family or friends

- we recognize that media professionals themselves may be affected by stories about suicide.

⦿ When supporting people after suicide, guide them towards safe communication strategies. In this way, postvention will become prevention.

⦿ There is a huge stigma and taboo about suicide. Sometimes people just don't know how to react. It is important to be aware that everyone will react differently after suicide.

⦿ All kinds of emotions may be present. If this leads to misunderstanding and conflict, mediation may help.

⦿ Some people leave suicide notes or messages. They will be treated as evidence during the investigation and released to the bereaved afterwards.

- Suicide notes come in many variations.

- If suicide notes contain aggressive or disturbing content, the bereaved sometimes choose not to view them.

- If suicide notes contain loving messages, they can be of comfort to the bereaved.

5

Breaking the Taboo: Religious and Cultural Perspectives, Guilt, and Shame after Suicide

This chapter will give a short historical timeline and describe perspectives from different religions on suicide. It will also introduce several philosophical and other views on suicide to give you a broader perspective. The second part of this chapter is about guilt and shame; you will read why it is important to work *with* guilt but *against* shame, and how this can be done during suicide postvention.

My search for answers

Rose and I were standing next to her son's body before it was covered to be taken for further investigation. The investigation of the scene where he died was finished and the police had told us that all the signs pointed to suicide. After this message was delivered, Rose turned very pale. Standing next to her son, she turned to me, took me by the shoulders in a tight grip, looked me in the eyes, and said in a frantic way, "Suicide is sinful. Andrea, will I see my son in heaven now? How can I know? I need to know!" In Rose's case, this was a question coming from a deeply religious person. And it was a very complicated question for me back then. I lacked the theological knowledge to give her an answer that was rooted in scriptures and theology. I called Rose's priest and he agreed to come over. I left soon after, but I took the question with me. And that is where my search for answers started.

Why is there such a huge taboo about suicide? Why is it so hard for us to talk about it?

Suicide can happen to anyone, anywhere. We all know someone who has lost someone or maybe even we have lost someone who died by suicide. We can identify with what happens and this makes suicide a scary subject to us; looking and even walking away, not thinking and talking about it may be more comfortable to us.

In looking at suicide, it is important to realize that the locus of conceptualization determines the way in which suicide is viewed by states, courts, religious leaders, and the public. This sounds very complicated, but it isn't. Basically, the locus of conceptualization is found by answering the why-question: Why does suicide happen? Where or with whom do we put the blame? Is suicide sinful?

Throughout history, these questions have been answered in many different ways; the locus of conceptualization has differed, and it still does—from lauding suicide as the necessary way to end one's life, to suicide as a major sin, and everything in between.

In ancient Greek society, suicide was often seen as the necessary thing to do. It was even applauded when famous or wealthy people died by suicide. Slaves and poor people were not allowed to die by suicide, though. That could become a costly business. Because people were seen as slaves, owned by others, suicide would cause the owners to lose valuable assets.

In ancient Rome, suicide was viewed in a neutral or even a positive way. Seneca wrote on the subject, stating that the quality of life was more important than its quantity. According to him, it was not only important to make sure you lived well, but also to die in a positive way.

Overview of suicide and the law

There is still a huge difference in the ways suicide is seen and handled across the world. In some countries, even attempting to end one's life is seen as a crime and people are sent to jail. If someone dies by suicide, some countries punish the bereaved or they ostracize bereaved people from communities. This may sound horrific, but don't forget that a country like the UK only relatively recently changed its law; until 1961, suicide was a crime in England and Wales. Prussia and France decriminalized it in 1751 and 1790 respectively.

You will still be able to find areas near Catholic cemeteries where people were buried after suicide, because Church law did not allow them to be buried in consecrated soil with others.

Some countries base their laws on religious laws; some countries use oppression or censorship to influence their population. In many countries, guilt and shame still influence the way suicide is seen.

Laws differ tremendously where suicide is concerned. Check your own country's regulations and laws on the subject. I can't possibly sum them all up. Even if I tried, the list would not be accurate as countries change their legislation.

While comparing laws on different continents and in different countries, you will also find contrary views. In my home country, the Netherlands, for example, there is a very open and liberal discussion about what is called the "right to die."

Some people will even argue that everyone should be allowed to die, that every individual has the right to decide. There are huge differences in views and opinions. Where do you stand? How do you feel about suicide? Do your views match policies in your country? There's no right or wrong answer, but just take some time to reflect on the above.

Do laws and religion influence suicide rates? Some headlines will tell you that religion is a protective factor where suicide is concerned.

Another angle is taken by sociologists. They argue that a strict regime will lower and more freedom will increase suicide risks.

You will also find science and the literature arguing, as suicide is such a complex subject.

And I wonder if it will ever be possible to fully compare suicide data and suicide rates from every continent and country. How and by whom are they registered? Will every suicide be reported if the consequences of reporting are so serious for those who stay behind?

Are all states and leaders transparent about suicide rates, willing to open up about this serious issue affecting their population?

We know that mental illness is a major factor in causing suicide, as science shows us. And we know that many people who die by suicide suffer constriction and an altered, narrowed worldview; they see the suicide as the only way to end their suffering. But they don't consciously choose death, because their thinking is influenced by their mental state.

How do systems based on restrictions, judging, and punishing influence this phenomenon? Can they?

So many questions and so few answers. So I will leave them here. I will go back to those I needed to answer to be able to do my work.

Rose's question, combined with observations I made while studying international laws and regulations, led me to pick up theology; it was easy to find regulations, rules, and (religious) laws, but what are they based on? How did we get to this taboo and all these aspects of guilt and shame surrounding suicide?

Religion and suicide

I will give you some background on how the major world religions view suicide. I apologize in advance that I won't cover them all, because that would take up too much space. The first part will be the longest; as a Christian, this happens to be the part I understand best. While teaching priests and clergy staff, I have found that it is important to share this knowledge. Take from this chapter what you need in your personal circumstances.

And be careful in judging and assuming.

My own assumptions

I remember the first time I was called to support bereaved people in a Muslim family, very early during my career. I went with many thoughts and, I will tell you honestly, I went with prejudice; How would I be accepted as a Christian woman? Looking back, my concerns were ridiculous and very wrong; here I was, with a mother and a father, brothers and sisters. Love and loss are universal when tragedy strikes, I learned. I did not know the specifics of their denomination and religious needs. So I just made that clear: "I am here for you, but you will have to guide me; my background is different to yours, so please let me know how I can help you best. And correct me if there are things you need me to do differently." The fact that suicide was seen as a sin by one of the family members was something I could relate to, even though my view was a different one; I was brought up around some very strict Church teachers, who had the same view on suicide as this family member. So I just listened, reflected, and mediated. Nowadays, we have extended training and colleagues from the Muslim community to guide us. But as a young crisis interventionist, I was on my own. I still look back to that call as a positive experience. It humbled me and I learned that assuming things to be a certain way causes prejudice; it was a wake-up call for me.

Abrahamic religions
Christianity

Being raised in a very strict Catholic setting, I remember very well how suicide was seen as sinful. Either it was not discussed or it was denied. Someone near and dear to me died by suicide. The next day we were told that the family wanted everyone to hear that he had died from a heart attack. I was basically told to lie about what had happened, because there was a tremendous amount of shame surrounding the death. I could not do that. I reported myself sick for school and I did not go to the funeral. A very sad memory for me, because I still feel I was robbed of the chance to say goodbye to someone important in my life.

It did not make sense to me, but as a child I did not question what I was told to do.

When Rose asked me the question I mentioned at the beginning of this chapter, she triggered my memory. And the many questions I had stuffed away in my brain required answers.

I heard what the Church said about suicide, but what did God say in the Bible? Oh my goodness, how He surprised me; I dove into the Bible and I found seven suicides, but I did not find the word "suicide" anywhere (that was added later in several translations). Furthermore, I did not find *any* condemnation in the Bible when the suicides were described.

So how did we get to the taboo and the condemnation of suicide?

We have to go a long way back in Church history; St Augustine (354–430 AD) addressed the subject of suicide in his first book of his "De Civitate Dei" series (a total of 22 books). His writings have been very important in Church doctrine ever since. Augustine did not use the word "suicide," but he had a strong opinion on ending one's life: it was against the will of God. He had a bit of difficulty with the story of Samson, and he could see how women could be tempted to end their life after rape, but all in all he condemned suicide.

The Church consequently changed Church law. In 452 AD, suicide was officially condemned. In 563 AD, it was decided that people who died by suicide should be refused Church burial rituals. In 693 AD, even a suicide attempt could lead to excommunication. In 860 AD, Pope

Nicolas I stated that suicide was a deadly sin. And in 1184 AD, the fact that suicide was a mortal sin was officially written in canon law.

Thomas Aquinas (1225–1274) later wrote about suicide, stating that it was a sin against God; God was the only one allowed to give and take life. This only added to the condemnation of suicide within the Church.

Martin Luther (1483–1546) tried to convince fellow Christians to be more compassionate towards suicidal people, but not many people were convinced by his view on the subject of suicide.

The philosopher Immanuel Kant (1724–1804) then opposed suicide, adding more fuel to the taboo fire.

Theologians Dietrich Bonhoeffer (1906–1945) and Karl Barth (1886–1968) saw how suffering could lead to suicide, but they felt that it could not be allowed and was against God's will. Their work was of great influence within both Catholic and Protestant Churches.

Centuries of writing condemning suicide got us to the huge taboo we often still experience nowadays. People within the Church followed Church guidance, and nobody seemed to notice that the Bible did not condemn suicide at all. This has led to many tragic situations and secondary damage.

Nowadays, the Church is more compassionate; people who die by suicide get a normal funeral in most church settings, and the bereaved are offered compassionate pastoral care. I have trained many priests and clergy colleagues. And they are making a difference to many.

Biblical suicides

With the exception of Samson's story, which was mentioned by some, the famous Christian writers did not really analyze the suicides in the Bible.

I think it is important to know where to find them and it is very interesting to look at them. Although the stories in the Bible were written a long time ago, they can offer us much food for thought.

I will quote Bible verses from the New International Version translation (NIV). If you want to dive deeper into this subject, I recommend you compare different translations and the Hebrew and Greek texts. It is interesting to study how translators interpret the suicides in the Bible; some are neutral, but some have even added the word "suicide" while translating.

Abimelech

> …a woman dropped an upper millstone on his head and cracked his skull. Hurriedly he called to his armor-bearer, "Draw your sword and kill me, so that they can't say, 'A woman killed him.'" So his servant ran him through, and he died. (Judges 9:53–54, NIV)

Technically, I could have left this death out. If you look at what happened, Abimelech died by what we would now call euthanasia or assisted dying. While studying this death in the Bible, my thoughts also wandered to cases we see nowadays, when desperate people get into situations where they provoke someone else to kill them. You may have heard of or maybe even encountered these "suicide by cop" situations.

In Abimelech's case (forced to grind grain), shame played a big part in his suicide; grinding grain was a woman's job, considered "too lowly" for men to perform. Oh, the things I would like to say about that, but I won't. Abimelech knew he was hurt and could die from his injuries. To prevent the shame of being killed by a woman, he arranged his own death.

Samson

> Samson said to the servant who held his hand, "Put me where I can feel the pillars that support the temple, so that I may lean against them." Now the temple was crowded with men and women; all the rulers of the Philistines were there, and on the roof were about three thousand men and women watching Samson perform. Then Samson prayed to the Lord, "Sovereign Lord, remember me. Please, God, strengthen me just once more, and let me with one blow get revenge on the Philistines for my two eyes." Then Samson reached toward the two central pillars on which the temple stood. Bracing himself against them, his right hand on the one and his left hand on the other, Samson said, "Let me die with the Philistines!" Then he pushed with all his might, and down came the temple on the rulers and all the people in it. Thus he killed many more when he died than while he lived. Then his brothers and his father's whole family went down to get him. They brought him back and buried him between Zorah and Eshtaol in the tomb of Manoah his father. (Judges 16:26–31, NIV)

I really think we need different wording, but if Samson had done what he did nowadays, he may just have made the headlines as a "suicide temple wrecker" or maybe even a "suicide terrorist"; he deliberately ended his life and planned to take many people with him. You may know his story; Samson had superpowers. And he was having trouble with the Philistines, killing many of them, after some personal issues. Looking for revenge and a way to overpower Samson, the Philistines went to Delilah, the girl Samson loved. She wanted to lure him into telling her about his superpowers. When Samson finally did, he told her that his hair held his superpower magic. When his hair was cut, his powers were gone. He was forced into slavery, spending every day on his knees grinding grain. The Philistines took out his eyes and made fun of him, making him to perform for an audience. Samson's suicide and consequent killing of many others was an act of revenge.

I deliberately included the last verse of the quotation because I think it is important: Samson's whole family came to pick him up and give him a proper funeral. In those days, family graves were only available to a very few rich people. The fact that Samson was buried in his father's grave means that he was treated with honor after death.

Bodies used to be put onto carved-out stone benches in caves, along with grave gifts, herbs, and perfumes. Decomposition would set in and the body would be left until only the bones remained. Then the bones and the gifts were collected in repositories and kept inside the grave.

What a difference if we compare this to practices based on religious rules, refusing to bury people who died by suicide in blessed soil, near the graves of near and dear ones. The Bible gives us a completely different example here!

Saul and his personal assistant

Now the Philistines fought against Israel; the Israelites fled before them, and many fell slain on Mount Gilboa. The Philistines pressed hard after Saul and his sons, and they killed his sons Jonathan, Abinadab and Malki-Shua. The fighting grew fierce around Saul, and when the archers overtook him, they wounded him critically.

Saul said to his armor-bearer, "Draw your sword and run me through, or these uncircumcised fellows will come and run me through and abuse me."

But his armor-bearer was terrified and would not do it; so Saul took his own sword and fell on it. When the armor-bearer saw that Saul was dead, he too fell on his sword and died with him. (1 Samuel 31:1–5, NIV)

A collective suicide

Here, Saul made a similar request to the one made by Abimelech. He basically asked his assistant to end his life before the enemy did. But the assistant was afraid, and Saul decided to end his own life. His assistant then copied Saul's behavior and followed him, dying in exactly the same way.

What follows in the story is what Saul feared; his body was damaged and put on public display in a horrible way by the Philistines. When others heard about this, they traveled to where the bodies of Saul and his sons were. They took them down and cremated them. The bones were then buried. Cremation was not customary back then, but it seems they used it here to avoid further abuse of the bodies of the deceased.

Again, the story ends with a respectful burial, followed by a period of fasting and mourning.

Ahithophel

Now in those days the advice Ahithophel gave was like that of one who inquires of God. That was how both David and Absalom regarded all of Ahithophel's advice…

Absalom and all the men of Israel said, "The advice of Hushai the Arkite is better than that of Ahithophel." For the Lord had determined to frustrate the good advice of Ahithophel in order to bring disaster on Absalom…

When Ahithophel saw that his advice had not been followed, he saddled his donkey and set out for his house in his hometown. He put his house in order and then hanged himself. So he died and was buried in his father's tomb. (2 Samuel 16:23, 17:14, 17:23, NIV)

I have added some verses leading up to Ahithophel's suicide; his advice used to be highly valued and important, but he was suddenly ignored. Did he feel useless, helpless, hopeless? Or was he ashamed of what had happened? There's a lot more information in this part of the Bible, but I'll leave the story here.

It is important to note (again!) that a proper burial in his father's tomb follows Ahithophel's death.

Zimri

> When the Israelites in the camp heard that Zimri had plotted against the king and murdered him, they proclaimed Omri, the commander of the army, king over Israel that very day there in the camp. Then Omri and all the Israelites with him withdrew from Gibbethon and laid siege to Tirzah. When Zimri saw that the city was taken, he went into the citadel of the royal palace and set the place on fire around him. So he died. (1 Kings 16:16–18, NIV)

Zimri had taken the royal throne in a coup, killing many people. When others found out, they overtook him. Instead of surrendering the palace to them, Zimri set the whole place on fire, including himself. The Bible follows this story by telling us that Zimri was a bad person. The texts condemn his actions during his lifetime, but his suicide is not commented upon or criticized. As with the other suicides, it is described in a neutral way—neither praised nor condemned.

Judas

> When Judas, who had betrayed him, saw that Jesus was condemned, he was seized with remorse and returned the thirty silver coins to the chief priest and the elders. "I have sinned," he said, "for I have betrayed innocent blood."
> "What is that to us?" they replied. "That's your responsibility."
> So Judas threw the money into the temple and left. Then he went away and hanged himself. (Matthew 27:3–5, NIV)

Judas felt remorseful and went back to the Sanhedrin. He had betrayed Jesus, pointing him out to the chief priests and elders by kissing him. I have heard this story over and over as a child and youngster; it was often depicted in movies and onstage. I always felt that these people, confronted with a desperate person, recognized his situation. They knew, because they would not even take back the money Judas came to return. It seemed to become almost toxic to them afterwards. And they practically said, "Bad luck, can't help you, go kill yourself." I know that is a harsh thing to write, but that is honestly what I feel when I study this passage. These people, the most important teachers and leaders in town behaved in this way.

My faith is about repentance and forgiveness. The opposite happened here; Judas is condemned. And he follows up by condemning and eliminating himself.

This is a very sad situation, but again the word "suicide" is not used, and the suicide is not condemned. Anywhere. Seven suicides in the Bible—no appraisal and no condemnation, just neutral reporting.

Later theology was based on other leads found in the Bible. Some theologians wrote that dying by suicide means you disobey the commandment that killing is not allowed.

Others have written that repentance is always possible in the eyes of God. So, technically, you could still go to heaven if you repented after sin. Suicide is a sin that ends your life. There is no opportunity left to repent, so you are doomed, some reasoned.

Funeral rites were withheld from people who died by suicide. The bereaved not only lost their loved one, they were actually shamed and punished afterwards, robbed of a proper and respectful way to say goodbye. Perhaps this would all make sense if nothing can be found in the Bible. But suicide *is* found, loving care for the body, and respectful funeral rites are described.

Lead by example. That's exactly what God showed us! If we believe the Bible to be God's Word and He mentions not one but seven suicides without condemnation, we should not add it ourselves!

Another Bible passage is important to share here because it shows us how a suicide is prevented.

About midnight Paul and Silas were praying and singing hymns to God, and the other prisoners were listening to them. Suddenly there was such a violent earthquake that the foundations of the prison were shaken. At once all the prison doors flew open, and everybody's chains came loose. The jailer woke up, and when he saw the prison doors open, he drew his sword and was about to kill himself because he thought the prisoners had escaped. But Paul shouted, "Don't harm yourself! We are all here!" The jailer called for lights, rushed in and fell trembling before Paul and Silas. (Acts 16:25–29, NIV)

The prison warder is so embarrassed that prisoners seemed to have escaped under his watch that he almost dies, because the shame of what happened triggered an impulse to end his life. But then there is Paul, actively practicing suicide prevention: *Do not harm yourself! We are all here!*

No condemnation, but support and help. A ministry of presence. Way to go, Paul!

Judaism

The three Abrahamic religions share several scriptures. Whole wars are based on differences, but we have so much in common as religions all rooted in Abraham.

Jewish views are mixed; Orthodox Jews consider suicide to be a sin, but many rabbinical scholars command compassion for both the deceased and the survivors.

There is no prohibition against suicide in the Talmud itself. The post-Talmudic tractate, Semahot (Ebel Rabbati) 2:1–5 served as the basis for most of later Jewish law on suicide, together with Genesis Rabbah 34:13, which bases the prohibition on Genesis 9:5.

I won't go into the above in detail because I am not a scholar in this field and scriptures are not very clear on the subject.

Jewish scriptures include written oral law; for example, in Tractate Bava Kama 91b, where it is written, "With regard to one who injures himself, although it is not permitted for him to do so, he is nevertheless exempt from any sort of penalty." It is written in a context where self-harm as a result of humiliation is being discussed.

But Jewish scholars also read Genesis chapter 6 as prohibiting the ending of one's life. Verse 5 is particularly important: "And surely your blood of your lives will I require." Jewish people believe that their body belongs to God and they are not allowed to hurt it. So suicide is condemned, and mourning rites should be withheld from people who died by suicide.

In reality this hardly ever happens, because Jewish Rabbis will find a reason for the death not to qualify as a suicide; most often the death is attributed to mental illness. The deceased will receive a traditional funeral and mourning rituals will be practiced.

Theologically, this is quite complicated, but the Jewish people I know all look at suicide with a great deal of compassion and care.

Islam

Suicide is strictly forbidden within Islam. Scriptures in the Qur'an clearly prohibit suicide.

Nor kill (or destroy) yourselves: for verily God hath been to you Most merciful! If any do that in rancor and injustice, soon shall we cast them into the Fire: and easy it is for God. (Qur'an 4:29–30)

Not only is suicide forbidden, but a punishment is added. In the Hadiths (written records of the words and actions of the Prophet), suicide is also condemned. Entrance to paradise is forbidden to people who die by suicide and punishment is described.

It is important to realize this when supporting Muslim people after suicide, but don't assume beforehand, as every case is different.

I have met some wonderful people from the Muslim community who supported the bereaved with compassion and great care. The body of the deceased was cared for by the parent, supported by others from the community. Prayers were said and the deceased's life remembered. Verses about a loving God were spoken, and intercessions for the deceased said.

But sometimes the opposite happens and there is judgment and condemnation of the death and the deceased. This often leads to very difficult and painful situations; loved ones have lost someone, and the death is followed by huge feelings of shame and guilt.

It is easy for us to condemn this; science and experience tell us that most people die by suicide in a state of severe mental illness. How can people judge a death that was not "chosen" in a healthy mental state?

I share these thoughts, but don't forget that Christian communities in our society used to treat the bereaved in very similar ways not too long ago. The difference is that the Bible does not provide a basis for these views. Islam scriptures do. I am not an expert on the Islamic faith, and I certainly don't have a theological solution here.

While responding to suicide calls, I try not to judge and just work within the circumstances; finding ways to connect in psychological alignment and support the bereaved, listening to them, reflecting, and helping them find ways to take control in their situation.

We meet these people on one of the darkest days of their lives. I feel that this is not the moment to march in with criticism of their beliefs and religious practice. Be kind. Be compassionate.

Suicide and terrorism

Since terrorism response is a subject I specialize in, I want to add a few sentences. Terrorism is performed by people with different ideologies;

these past years we have seen right-wing, left-wing, and Jihadi terrorists causing horrible harm.

Suicide prevention colleagues from the Middle East recently voiced their concern about media headlines combining the words "suicide" and "terrorism." They are fighting taboo and stigma while working in suicide prevention in Muslim countries. If you have read the section above, you will understand how complicated their work is.

We currently see many headlines on "suicide terrorism"—terrorists taking their own life while ending the lives of as many others as possible. This way of reporting only increases the stigma and taboo about suicide, and Muslim theology does not support adding the two together.

> ...if any one slew a person—unless it be for murder or for spreading mischief in the land—it would be as if he slew the whole people: and if any one saved a life, it would be as if he saved the life of the whole people. (Qur'an 5:32)

I have added this here because I don't have a simple solution to the point made by our international colleagues, but I feel we should all be considerate. We need to see if we can find solutions, because together we know and can do so much more.

Indian religions

Both Hinduism and Jainism condemn suicide. It is seen as sinful and unacceptable, because life is sacred.

There are certain insights on practices such as fasting till death, but in modern theory we would call this a subintentional death and not suicide.

In Buddhism, people can be born again, and it is believed that past deeds influence present experiences; this is called karma. So one's current suffering could be a consequence of past deeds. Although the destruction of life (and therefore suicide) is not allowed, it is not condemned in Buddhism.

There are some writings about monks who died by suicide, but it is said that they were not yet enlightened, as a higher state of Buddhism is described; suicide is an exception, according to Buddhist writings.

Pagan religions

Many different groups are put into this category: Druidism, Wicca and Shamanism among them.

I did not really find a consensus on the subject of suicide among them, and there is not one book or collection of scriptures to study on the subject.

Generally, within paganism, life is seen as sacred and it should not be taken. As reincarnation is something that will follow death, suicide is consequently not something that will lead to a different "final state"; life starts and ends and starts again in a continuum.

So while taking one's life could be seen as a violation or a lack of honoring the sanctity of life, people who believe in these religions will feel that they will return and get another chance to cope with life.

I apologize if I have missed any religions or certain aspects within the religions above. To me, I have found that this information is sufficient to assist me in my work.

We have some amazing colleagues from different religious communities within our teams. They advise us and help us to refer when necessary.

In many countries, wonderful organizations from many different religions can be found if a more specific referral is needed. Go online and check out the availability in your country and region.

Philosophical views and other insights

Suicide has been researched and written about from many different angles; sociologists, psychologists, psychiatrists, epidemiologists, historians, and biologists all try to grasp this complex issue.

Studying these different angles will give you a better understanding of suicide, but not a full one.

Suicide is major and massive problem in our society. While the Church kept condemning suicide, Enlightenment thinkers made efforts to explain it.

Jean-Jacques Rousseau (1712–1778) wrote about suicide that the locus of blame (and therefore the sinful part of suicide) should not be with the person who died, but with society causing the person to become and act the way he did. Nobody is born suicidal, but society can make a person become suicidal.

David Hume (1711–1776) made an effort to decriminalize suicide. In 1777 he wrote an essay called "On suicide," but it was so controversial that not everyone was allowed to read it. He wrote that people were making way too big a deal about suicide. It should not be viewed as an act of sinning against God.

You can find a lot of literature on the subject and I can't go into all of it. I will just add two important views.

First is Sigmund Freud (1856–1939). Having studied psychiatric nursing, I can tell you that I don't belong to the Freud fan club, but his work is still an important part of our education.

Freud placed suicide and its causes inside the suicidal mind, which was a new way to look at it; Freud said that the person did not consciously kill themselves during suicide. But he thought that the suicide was actually a battle fought inside the mind that was projected onto the person's own body; in psychodynamics, this is called "murder in the 180th degree"; while cutting their own body with a knife, for example, Freud thought the person was actually acting out a battle from within the mind with a person from the suicidal person's past.

Simply put, the person physically put the knife into his own body, but mentally attacked the other person. This theory has since been picked up and modified by others.

Another important theory on suicide is the social approach taken by French sociologist Émile Durkheim (1858–1917) in his 1897 book *Le Suicide*. Durkheim explained the causes of suicide by examining the relationship between the suicidal person and society.

He determined three types of suicide. *Altruistic* suicide is required and requested by society, according to Durkheim. Customs, or sometimes even rules, may leave a person no choice, and, when he dies by suicide, his death is praised. An example of altruistic suicide is Harakiri or Seppuku, a ceremonial way of ending one's life from Japan.

In *egoistic* suicide, a person disconnects from society and the people around them. I explained *constriction* earlier; a suicidal person's worldview becomes very narrow. They experience only suffering and, in tunnel-vision-like circumstances, death becomes a solution to end their suffering. Looking at their situation from a broader or different perspective has become impossible. Society is not reaching the person and the person does not know how to connect society. Attachment is lost. Most suicides in Western society would be categorized by Durkheim as egoistic.

I see what he means, but to me the word has a very negative connotation and I don't use it when working with responders or the bereaved.

Durkheim's third category of suicide is *anomic* suicide. An extreme situation occurs, such as the loss of a loved one or of all material possessions. This feels like an immediate loss of all ties to society and a person dies by suicide. A syntax error occurs in the life of a person, causing them to immediately feel completely lost. When we talk about *impulse* suicides, this is what we mean. I haven't seen too many of these cases, but they do happen.

A split-second decision

Recently an employee was fired by his manager. He walked out of the office, took the staircase to the roof, and jumped. He died before his manager had officially filed the paperwork on the dismissal. A split second, but everything was lost to those the employee left behind.

I could write a whole book on different views on suicide. If you wish to explore the subject further, there are books listed in the Resources section. Much research is being done on the genes and brains of people who have died by suicide; the researchers' reasoning is that if we can find a gene or a certain brain structure, we may be able to prevent suicide.

The downside of these studies (and the headlines they receive) is the stress and worry they may cause in those affected.

Online stressors

Dan was left behind with three young children, all under the age of 6. I had been with them on the day of the suicide and was asked to go back the next day. Dan had gone online and found many links, describing how suicide runs in families. He was convinced that suicide was hereditary, and he started panicking, looking at his three children; their mother died by suicide, so their risk of dying by suicide was massive, he concluded. I asked Dan to show me the computer. Many tabs in his browser were open. He closed them one by one, and we had a long talk about his wife and their children. I explained the science but added the many prevention options and strategies we know. The headlines and Doctor

Google combined with the acute stress (Dan's wife had only just died) influenced his way of thinking. I gave him some stress management techniques. I later heard that Dan had visited a psychiatrist a few weeks after his wife's death. He was able to ask all of his questions and received specific advice. Dan's children are teenagers now, and he is supporting others bereaved by suicide. He informs them about risks, but never without options and solid prevention advice.

Before I continue, I recommend the work of research professor Brené Brown. She has written several amazing books and you can find many open-access videos explaining difficult subjects in an amazing and very helpful way.

As I write this, her YouTube video on empathy has been watched almost 10 million times! She explains how empathy is all about psychological alignment, about a non-judgmental ministry of presence—supporting others in times of need, being there with them and for them. We can't change their difficult circumstances, but we can let them feel that they are not alone.

Empathy connects us with the other person. Without it, suicide postvention is better left to others.

Guilt and shame

Brené Brown has done a lot of research on guilt and shame. After suicide, many complex feelings emerge. And guilt and shame are big factors in the process. Brown explains the difference between guilt and shame in a very simple way: Guilt puts the focus on behavior, and shame puts the focus on the person. Guilt says, "I *made* a mistake." Shame says, "I *am* a mistake." Guilt is uncomfortable, but it comes with the ability to help us to correct our ways, changing things for the better. Shame only has negative side effects and nothing good can ever come from it.

It is important to note that Brown found a way to handle shame: if shame is put into words and spoken about, it loses its power. If you talk about shame, you are actively diminishing it. Try it; it really works.

More people have spoken and written about guilt, but I am a big fan of Brown's work. She breaks very complicated issues down into very small and clear pieces.

Guilt and shame have always been prominent in the cases I worked on. As human beings, we tend to correct others when they voice feelings of guilt: "Oh, come on, this is not your fault. Stop blaming yourself." Feelings of shame, on the other hand, are often ignored; we don't know what to say and change the subject if we see that the other person feels ashamed or embarrassed.

Actively working with guilt and shame should be a part of every postvention training; we are often not aware and mean well, but *well meant is not automatically well done.*

During roleplay and exercises, we can investigate our own "modus operandi" to recognize unproductive habits and replace them in a safe setting. I still learn so much while teaching and training, and I will probably continue to be a lifelong learner myself.

It is important to learn that during suicide postvention work, we work *with* guilt, but we work *against* shame.

Working with guilt

Throughout this book, you have read how control is an antidote to despair. Suicide often causes feelings of despair, hopelessness, and helplessness. And the question always comes up: *Why?* The only person who could have answered is no longer around to do so.

While looking for ways to cope with the situation, people try to take control. Taking on guilt can be a coping strategy to the bereaved, and it may not make any sense to us, as outsiders. A whole guilt construct may be set up in the mind, which may seem completely irrational. But it isn't; *guilt makes sense.*

We need to acknowledge it, be very careful to touch it and don't just try to take it away; you may be taking away a coping strategy.

Yvonne, 39, who lost her teenage daughter to suicide

I had hit the alarm clock and fallen back to sleep that morning. If I hadn't, she would still be around. My phone was offline, and I normally turn it on when I get out of bed. She must have looked at my WhatsApp messenger and seen that my phone had been offline since 11 pm. It normally is online from 7 am, but that day I only turned it on at 8, when I woke up. She died on the railway tracks at 7.50 am, the police told me. If I had been available, if I had been online, she would have messaged me. I know she would have. I could have saved her. I should have saved her.

Yvonne was very clear from the beginning; we arrived at her house with the police not long after the death to inform her. She was devastated, but she immediately took on the guilt and blame for her daughter's death.

Yvonne continued

The young police officer who had delivered the message had a really hard time dealing with this situation. Since there were two of us, crisis interventionists, my colleague discreetely asked the police officer to step out with him. We met him later at the police station and had tea together. The situation had been new and overwhelming to him. We listened and could give him some background information and tools. Our talk was not registered and remained confidential, which is so very important. Two weeks later, I happened to meet the officer at another incident. And I was happy to hear that he was doing well. He thanked me for what had started off as a horrible day but ended with a good conversation and a positive frame; he felt more confident and had evaluated Yvonne's case with his superior, who had complimented him on his work.

So what do you do when guilt is taken on? You handle it with care; you first look at it and study it. Don't just take it away, let it be.

Yvonne continued

Yvonne kept going back to her morning and was convinced her daughter would still be alive if she had gotten up earlier. "Yvonne, listening to you I hear that you are blaming yourself for what happened." "Yes, it's my fault she died," Yvonne said.

Reading this may make you uncomfortable; here's a mother in a horrific situation, apparently making it even worse for herself.

And this is exactly how this situation feels when you encounter it for the first time. I recommend you practice situations like this one in roleplay. You can't and shouldn't copy my words or anyone else's; confronted with difficult situations, you will have to find your own words and strategies. You are your instrument; be genuine. In Yvonne's case, I just reflected on her feelings.

We usually see that during the days and weeks after the death, stress hormones reduce and people regain a broader level of cognitive functioning; other coping strategies are found and people automatically start to look at their situation from different perspectives. Talking with others may help. Yvonne found support in a peer group for bereaved people.

Yvonne continued

After the second meeting, I decided to stop beating myself up. My thinking seemed to become more clear, and I felt ridiculous: What was I thinking? It felt like I had to take a step forward; I had to accept what had happened; my child had ended her life. And she left me out. She had decided to go alone. That reality hit me. It hit me hard. I broke down in tears and cried a river. But that river needed to start flowing. It was about time it did.

In other cases, I may ask, "I hear you are experiencing feelings of guilt. What could you have done differently?" Often the answer will be "Nothing."

But sometimes situations pose different challenges.

Philip's father, different kinds of guilt

Philip had died after a fight with his father. His last words to his father had been "I will just go and kill myself." Philip drove his car on to the highway, driving against traffic. He steered towards a lorry and died on impact. We did not know this when we went out to inform his next of kin; the incident was handled as a traffic collision that needed further investigation. The lorry driver was injured and unable to answer questions. Witnesses arrived after the crash, so the circumstances were unclear to us at that time. Philip lived at his parents' house and he had carried his ID. Both his father and mother were present when we brought them the terrible news.

Philip's father had an immediate physical reaction; he almost collapsed and had to vomit.

The police officers explained to the parents that an investigation into the collision would be done, which would take a while. Philip's body would be examined.

Guilt showed up in many ways in Philip's case: *objective* guilt. Philip had caused a deadly traffic incident; in a legal sense, he was *responsible* for what happened.

This could have turned into a challenging situation. In this case, Philip's parents were very open. The police had questions and his mother answered them honestly. Depending on the country of residence, her answers might have had major consequences for legal insurance decisions that could follow. Some people choose not to answer questions. It's important that they are informed about their rights and any consequences. That is not our job, as suicide postventionists. The police will inform people and officers are trained to do so.

However, it is important to keep an eye on the wellbeing of the people we are supporting; we have been working closely with the police for years, so officers will often ask our advice when it has to be determined whether people are "fit for questioning."

Sometimes they aren't; a situation can be so overwhelming that people are just not able to answer questions.

Philip's mother could answer the questions the police officer had. He left to join his colleagues and we stayed.

While the police colleagues were investigating the incident and looking at objective guilt, in this case we also encountered a huge amount of subjective guilt, while supporting his parents; they felt responsible for what had happened. They should have prevented it, they thought.

Philip's father continued

We had heard what had happened that morning, because the mother had explained it to the police officer. Father and son had often had major conflicts and the son had threatened to "kill himself" before. He had left the house in a very angry mood.

The father was physically unwell and did not say a word while the police colleague was around. After the officer left, an uncomfortable tension developed between the parents.

When we enter a home with the most horrific news, we are invading a very private area. In Philip's case, I really sensed that. But I also felt that it was important to be there for both parents.

My colleague asked the mother to tell him about her son. They got up and walked through the house, looking at pictures and items important to her.

I stayed with the father and closed the door to allow us some privacy. I repeated how sorry I was for his loss. And that I felt so sorry to hear about the way they had parted that morning.

I hadn't even finished my sentence when words burst from the father's mouth. It felt as if I had just opened up a bottle under pressure—catharsis.

At first his words and sentences were incoherent so I just listened. After a while he was able to take a deep breath, and I was able to reflect with him.

There was nothing I could do to change anything about the situation; it was what it was. It was raw and too heavy to carry for him. Psycheache. Grief, guilt, and a lamenting father, begging God to turn back time, so he could change the situation and tell his son how precious he was to him.

A ministry of presence was all I could offer.

Philip's father was a religious person. After a long talk, we called his priest who immediately came over and stayed with the parents when we left. The father was referred to a therapist. He has received one-to-one support and both parents see the therapist together regularly.

When we hear police colleagues discuss guilt, they often mean objective guilt. And it is important to keep that in mind. After suicide, *subjective* guilt plays a big role; people *experience* and *feel* guilt. Although Philip steered the car, his father *felt* responsible.

His mother had an even more complex response. On the one hand, she felt she should have stopped her son from getting into the car. Could she have taken away his car keys? Could she have intervened? She was asking herself many questions. And, on the other hand, there was anger, towards both father and son, for not being able to control themselves and arguing in a very aggressive way.

If you run into complicated guilt situations, it is important to look at the guilt. Are you dealing with objective guilt? Or is it subjective guilt that you are encountering? There may be an ongoing investigation to see if objective guilt can be established: Was there a crime and can/must someone be held responsible for this crime? Difficult questions may need to be asked, but a thorough investigation will benefit everyone in the end, even if it doesn't feel that way in the immediate aftermath.

While supporting people, it can sometimes be necessary to differentiate between subjective and objective guilt. This sounds complicated, but it isn't, because you can ask specific questions to get a clear perspective:

- If you had known what would happen, would you have done what you did?

- Did you intend for this to happen? Did you mean to cause these consequences?

These questions will help you while supporting people, even if objective guilt is being investigated. When the investigative part (the questioning) is finished, you can really help to make sense of complicated feelings by asking these questions.

Just make sure you don't fill in the answers. Listen and reflect; never assume.

The questions above may also help you when guilt is imposed, either by the deceased or by others.

Kerry's sister

Kerry's sister had died from a gunshot wound to the face and head. Kerry had found her. Not only had the image had startled her, she also found several notes with very angry messages to her and the rest of the family; Kerry's sister blamed her family for her death.

Dan's girlfriend

Dan found his girlfriend's body at her apartment. They were having severe relationship issues, because Dan had had an affair with a co-worker. She had been suffering from depression. Her parents found out about the affair. After their daughter's death, they immediately blamed Dan for what happened. They declared that he would not be allowed to enter the funeral home and he would not be welcome at the funeral.

These are painful and difficult situations. We sometimes become mediators during the aftermath, but we have to be very careful and respect people's opinions and decisions; it's not up to us to actively intervene.

Working these cases is tough. It can be very helpful to reflect on them with colleagues, either in an intervision team meeting or in personal supervision. There are no protocols, no scripts for this important ministry-of-presence work.

In Kerry's case, a strong family bond and support from a bereavement charity helped them to get through the first very difficult days.

In Dan's case, relationships were so complicated that he was not able to go to his girlfriend's funeral. Her parents were supported by different colleagues. We did manage to arrange an opportunity for him to visit the funeral home for a private viewing. Her parents agreed to that. It was a small opening in an extremely complicated situation.

And we can only do so much. Pastoral support may help in some cases, but other cases may need referral to professional therapeutic support.

Guilt and children

I asked you above to handle guilt with care and not to take it away, as it can be part of a person's coping strategy.

When children are bereaved, guilt requires a different approach and some extra attention. I recommend that you check out the websites of charities in your own country; each country has amazing organizations specializing in support for bereaved children. Some even offer expertise to help children after suicide.

Inform yourself and browse around; when you are responding, there is no time to explore. Do it now and have some links and downloads available to use when needed.

Many theories on cognitive development in children can be found. Here's how I look at it: children are the sun in their own solar system. The people and events they encounter are like planets floating past. As in every solar system, the sun is influencing everything moving around it. So a child looks at people and situations while explaining everything from within. This can almost become like magical thinking: "I am the one influencing everything that happens." When bad things happen, causality is sought within: Children look for the blame within themselves; they are guilty of what happened.

Kevin's conclusion

Kevin had been sitting quietly on a chair since we arrived. He was looking pale and did not move a lot. I asked him to show me around and tell me about his dad. I had taken a candle from my bag and asked Kevin to find me a nice picture of his dad and a good spot to put both the candle and the picture to remember him. Kevin started to cry when we were in the hallway. We sat down on the stairs together. Kevin told me about a fight he and his dad had last Easter. It was now almost Christmas, but Kevin told me about the fight as if it had happened yesterday; he had not cleaned up his room and wouldn't listen to his mom. When his dad came home, he had opened Kevin's closet door and found crisps and candy Kevin had "stolen" from the basement. His dad had gotten very angry and had shouted, "Kevin, I am under so much stress right now. I can't have this now. You are killing me." And here we were, on the stairs. And Kevin had killed his dad, as he had predicted. At least, that was the way Kevin felt. We had a long talk and managed to find a different perspective together. Before we left, I got the family an appointment with a bereavement support group specializing in support to children bereaved by suicide.

Supporting Eva

Eva had performed CPR on her grandfather. The doctor arrived quickly and just pushed Eva away. He assessed the situation and pronounced Eva's grandfather dead immediately. While doing a first quick physical examination, he said, "Ah, ribs are broken." Eva heard that and ran to her room. Her mom took me to her. She was sitting in a corner, her knees against her chest and her head down.

I introduced myself and asked if it would be OK if I sat down next to her. She was shivering. I covered her with a blanket. We just sat there for a while. And slowly we managed to find each other in a conversation. Eva had learned CPR at school. I complimented her for the way she had responded, but she answered angrily that she had felt her grandpa's ribs crack under her hands. And the doctor had said they were broken. So she killed her grandpa. She was convinced it was her fault he died.

I told her I would be right back and went down to the doctor, who was filling out some paperwork. I explained and he came upstairs with me. He explained to Eva that ribs often break when CPR is performed. He told her it had happened to him. And he added how scary it had felt under his hands. Eva nodded. The doctor then explained that she had done everything just right; if there had been any possibility of saving her grandpa, that would have happened. But the doctor told Eva he had examined him and could tell that he had been dead for a while. Nobody could have saved him. I asked Eva to find us a nice sheet to cover grandpa, because the doctor had to take his body for some tests he could only perform at the hospital. The police officers had finished their work and allowed Eva to have some time with her grandpa, who was put on a gurney. She covered him with the colored sheet she had brought downstairs and she helped wheel the gurney out to the car.

The two cases above are just two examples of what I have seen while supporting children. Their rationale may seem simplistic to you, but if these issues are not addressed, they can become a massive stumbling block in the healing and recovery process. Observe children, listen to them, read between the lines. And don't be afraid to ask; work with them. Sometimes, with children, guilt needs to be challenged.

Working against shame

While guilt is about behavior, shame is not. Shame is about blaming oneself; remember how I wrote above that guilt says you *did something bad* while shame says you *are* bad. Shame puts the focus on the person. Although shame can have a huge impact, working with shame is not complicated; we know how to take away its power: talk about it and tackle it. As soon as shame is spoken about, its power diminishes.

Shame does not have any positive side effects. It is damaging in many ways. And we don't need further damage in an already devastating situation.

Shame after suicide is very common; suicide is surrounded by taboo and people are often worried about how others may respond or view them when they find out a loved one took their own life. This can even lead to situations where a different cause of death is mentioned to the outside world, as I had to experience when someone I knew died.

Or it can lead to people avoiding contact, isolating themselves, afraid of what others might say or think if they met. Our minds can make up stories as soon as we start to assume what might happen and these stories can become very negative and harmful.

Sometimes people will cross the street or turn away from someone bereaved by suicide; they often don't know what to say, so they may avoid contact. This can lead to a massive increase in feelings of shame.

In supporting people while responding after suicide, it is important to separate feelings of guilt and feelings of shame; to the bereaved, all of these feelings may be experienced as one huge pile of mind clutter. We can help them by reflecting on these feelings.

How to work with guilt was discussed above.

If you encounter shame, it is important to talk about this with the bereaved. Don't make it complicated; confront and challenge the shame you see. For example:

> "I hear you say that you feel you don't want to tell anyone. What would happen if you did?"
>
> "Well, everyone would know and talk about it. I am a healthcare professional, and nobody would ever take me seriously again—they would see me as incompetent."
>
> "OK, so let's look at it differently. If you heard that a colleague's partner had suffered from mental illness and died by suicide, would you look at the colleague as an incompetent healthcare professional?"
>
> Silence.
>
> "Well, no, of course not…"
>
> Silence.
>
> "So why is this different in your situation?"

Shame just lost a lot of its power. And if you continue to talk about it, reflecting and looking for action perspectives together, it will diminish even more.

It is easy to test and practice this in everyday situations. Try it; it works!

Day-to-day shame

I recently had surgery on my head. My hair was covered in blood and I was not allowed to wash it for a few days. But I had to work when I was called to assist in a crisis situation. I could not think of any way to make my hair look decent. So I went into the meeting and started off saying, "Listen, everyone, I know I look horrible, but I am fine. I had some minor surgery and am not allowed to wash my hair. Please forgive me for looking like a scarecrow."

My shame lost its power and we could concentrate on the work.

Shame and postvention

Molly, tackling shame together

Molly lived in a very religious community. Her brother had moved in with her because he was suffering from a mental illness and was not able to live on his own. His suicide did not come as a surprise, but Molly was deeply saddened. She owned the local grocery store and panicked when she thought about going to work; "everyone will know, they will all be talking about me, they will all be staring at me." She had quite extreme expectations about what would happen. I knew the community and understood what she meant; there were indeed some elderly people with some very rigid views on life. We looked at options and strategies. Molly was building a huge image in her mind and I suggested that she just take the bull by the horns; we went over to her store. She called her staff into the office and told them straight out what happened; "Sam died last night. He ended his own life." There were no strange looks, but hugs and tears followed. She told the staff that she was worried about people's opinions and judgment. Indeed, there were some confrontations with customers walking up to her, making blunt comments. Her staff were always near to defuse the situation and had Molly's back.

CHAPTER 5—SUMMARY

- There is a huge amount of stigma and taboo related to suicide.

- In some parts of the world suicide is seen as a crime.

- In the Western world, suicide was decriminalized during the 20th century.

- While suicide was not condemned in the ancient Greek and Roman world, it became a crime in the fifth century AD.

- This was influenced by Church writers such as St Augustine and Thomas Aquinas, but in my opinion was not supported by biblical descriptions of suicide.

- The Bible describes seven suicides, but it does not condemn suicide anywhere; on the contrary; it even gives us a suicide prevention strategy.

- In other world religions, suicide is not allowed or encouraged, but it is also not condemned.

- An exception is found within Islam; in the Muslim world, scriptures clearly forbid suicide. It is important to know this if you are supporting Muslim people after suicide. But never assume certain reactions or responses; always work in psychological alignment and be respectful. Don't judge.

- The social sciences have brought us many different views on suicide; Rousseau, Freud, and Durkheim are a few important names to mention and know.

- Guilt and shame are often present after suicide. As Brené Brown noted, it is important to differ between them.

- Guilt puts a focus on behavior: "I *made* a mistake." Shame puts a focus on a person: "I *am* a mistake."

- Guilt may be a coping strategy. It is important to work with it.

- Shame never has positive aspects. It is important to work against it. Shame loses power when it is put into words.

- If children are involved and they are feeling guilt or shame, it can be helpful to ask for expert advice on how to support them.

6

Special Cases of Suicide

This chapter will describe several different kinds of cases we encounter while working in suicide postvention. You will read about children and suicide, about suicide clusters, combined suicides, murder-suicide and suicide by cop. There is a short section on famous people's suicides, and I have added information about suicide on cruise ships. The final section of this chapter will consider specific incidents I have encountered; it will include some basic information about autoerotic fatalities and my thoughts on a suicide in an international courtroom.

By now you will have read about the complexity and difficulty suicide poses, but sometimes we are called to cases that are even more difficult. This chapter discusses a few examples. They provide extra challenges, and expert advice and guidance may be needed. Know they can happen and don't hesitate to ask for help and support, should you encounter them.

Children and suicide

As I have explained, finding ways to regain control is an antidote to feelings of hopelessness and helplessness. Not just in adults, but also in children. What we often see in crisis intervention is that parents want to protect their children by leaving them out during difficult moments and decisions. This is very understandable, but we have seen that this is often not the best way to react when children are bereaved by suicide.

Even very young children have a need to be seen and heard. And by involving them in rituals and giving them action perspectives, we are helping them deal with the situation. Children will have their own understanding of death, depending on their age. A very young child will experience longing and missing. A kindergarten-aged child may talk about someone being dead, but not really understand what it means. A primary school child may start to understand the permanent nature of the loss. During the early teenage years, a full understanding will grow while the child's brain develops.

If you are working with children, there are excellent books to be found, which go into more detail about child development and grief reactions. For me, it is important to advise you to involve the children when supporting a family after suicide. But that doesn't mean it is appropriate to have them present every step of the way.

Boundaries

The younger the child, the more important their bonding to their caregiver is, especially during stressful situations; a toddler will be very responsive to the emotions its mother may experience. Since every person and every case is different, I cannot give you a fixed protocol here. If there is a damaged relationship between the child and its caregiver, or if the deceased was the only caregiver in a child's life, you will have to work from there. Get specialist advice if you feel it is needed.

What I have learned is that sadness and grief are familiar reactions to a child; tears and sadness will come and go, like waves during a storm. A child's natural behavior in a healthy child–parent bond will be to try to comfort its caregiver. If this happens, I just let the parent and the child ride out the waves together.

I often talk about a major storm at sea when speaking about the immediate aftermath and suicide bereavement; the waves are so very high that you can't see the land. That's why lighthouses were invented—even during a storm we will be able to see the lighthouse and find direction. A child needs a lighthouse and young children will look for direction from their caregivers.

It's OK to see and feel that the caregiver is grieving. And it can be very powerful if the child and the caregiver can find comfort in each other's presence. But sometimes the acute stress will lead to severe reactions in the caregiver, causing (temporary) dysfunction. They may not be emotionally or physically available to the child. This situation is unknown and unfamiliar to the child, and it can be very scary. Caregivers may push the child away. Or there may be panic or aggressive behavior; these are normal reactions to an extreme situation, but we can't explain this to a very young child. If this situation occurs, we may need to support the parent and the child separately for a while.

It is important to help the parent to find ways to regain control and functioning, and we need to provide safety and comfort to the child. If there is no known caregiver available, we will be the ones to provide it. Be a lighthouse.

Shelley's son, finding safety

Shelley's husband had died by suicide. We went over to her house to inform her about the death. She was at home with her 3-year-old son. Shelley had a very emotional reaction to the information. She was screaming and very upset. And she started to hit the table, using her fists. Her little boy first watched her in silence and then showed similar behavior, screaming very loudly. I looked at my colleague and we agreed without words what would happen next. I picked up the boy and went upstairs. We found his room which was a safe place for him, and closed the door. The little boy was very confused, but he calmed down after a while. When I heard that the situation downstairs had become calmer, I did a quick check and took the boy back downstairs. Shelley was now sitting down, crying. Her boy ran towards her and crawled on to her lap.

The days leading up to the funeral may be very stressful to the bereaved. Whenever I am concerned about a situation, I try to see if there is a trusted person in the child's life who is available to offer support specifically to them. I will look for someone who is not directly bereaved by the loss themselves. This may be a known babysitter, a daycare leader, a neighbor, a friend's parent, or another person trusted by the child. These people are usually very happy to help.

Shelley's son continued

When asked who we could call to help Shelley's little boy, she gave us Jane's phone number. Jane was her little boy's daycare mom while

Shelley worked. Jane immediately came over, and it was good to see how safe the little boy felt around her. Together, we made a plan for the days leading up to the funeral: the boy would be with Jane during the usual hours, and Shelley could call her 24/7, should she need support.

Jane sat next to the boy at the funeral. At one moment, when Shelley became very upset, Jane walked out with the boy. They took a small walk and went back in after a short while. When music was played, he got up and danced next to the coffin. The funeral was recorded and photographed, and a few flowers were dried and framed with a picture of the daddy. Should the son ask questions later on, Shelley would be able to explain and show him how they said goodbye together.

When children are older, they will be able to understand and take part more. If you are responding to a suicide and the situation makes it necessary that children leave the incident scene for a while, never just send them to their room; always make sure they find an action perspective. This will help them take control. Explain who is present, who will be coming, and what will happen next.

Helping children take control

The German doctor asked us to leave the room because she was about to start the medical examination of the body. The mother was asked to answer a detective's questions in the kitchen. The police requested that the children went upstairs. I went with them. The children were aged 6 to 12 and had many questions. I asked them to find a picture of their dad and took out a candle from my backpack. We lit it and I asked them to tell me about him: "I can see how special your daddy is to you and I wish I could have met him before. But I can't now. So please tell me about him." Tears were shed, but they also retrieved some funny memories.

I then explained to them what would happen next: The doctor would take daddy's body to the hospital to examine it some more. They would be allowed to see him before the doctor left. One of the children had been in an ambulance, so I could explain that daddy's body would be put on a similar stretcher, but one with a cover. And that it would be taken away in a van. The stretcher and the van looked dark and gray, so I suggested we could find something nice to cover it; they had told me how bright daddy was, so wouldn't it be great to find a sheet or blanket in bright colors? The children decided on a blanket. I took it downstairs, with the eldest child. The cover was already closed. We put the blanket over it and had the other children come down. Later, during the viewing, the blanket was washed and put on a rocking chair in the room. After the funeral, the rocking chair and the blanket were put in a corner of the living room. It is a spot the children love to use to remember or just read a book.

Teenagers are very worldly-wise nowadays; they have often seen films or the *CSI* series on TV, and have really surprised me by asking the most complicated questions. They live in an in-between phase: they behave in very adult ways on the one hand, but they are also vulnerable, young, and inexperienced on the other hand. Working through suicide bereavement while you are experiencing a strange phase of hormone madness is incredibly tough. I lost someone close to me when I was 16, so I know how devastating this can be.

Teenagers are often treated in very childish ways after a suicide. This may be well meant, but not always well done. Take teens seriously—they can handle more information than you think. Ask them what they need. Listen and psychologically align, even if this is difficult for you and me, as oldies. Teenagers often feel comfortable around peers. Don't jump in too soon, but when you are called to a bereaved teen, think ahead and see if there are peer bereavement groups in the area. Get the information and offer it to the teenager at a later stage.

Tim, 15, who lost his dad to suicide

I was called to Tim (15) because he had been in bed for 18 hours after the news was brought. He did not talk and his uncle was worried about him. Tim's dad had used a gun to end his life. I went into his room and introduced myself. I did not get a response. I asked Tim if it would be OK if I sat down on the chair in his room. He nodded. I just sat there, which is really hard; enduring the silence is something that really needs focus. After a while there was a moment of curiosity in Tim's attention. I caught his look and immediately followed up with a question. After a short while we were in an active conversation.

Tim had overheard a lot of information, even though he had been in his room. He couldn't stop imagining what his dad must have thought. He wanted to know which gun his dad used and how he used it. Was his brain still in his head? Was it painful? Did he die immediately?

I answered him honestly. And I asked him to write down the questions I could not answer. Tim felt "like a freak" for wondering about these things. I told him he was a normal kid having normal thoughts after something extreme had happened to him. A detective later answered Tim's questions.

The psychological alignment in Tim's case wasn't easy; when people are withdrawn, it is hard to find them. But there will be small opportunities, like the moment Tim looked at me. If you miss these tiny windows, it may be a long time before another opportunity is given. It is not something Tim consciously did. It is just something that happens. I have sat with many children in similar situations. I have worked using a child's pet as mediator; pets will be experiencing stress too. If the child does not respond, I may start to talk to the pet. Children will often join in. Be creative; you are your own instrument.

Suicide clusters

Earlier I wrote about the contagion that may occur when people are triggered by another suicide and become suicidal themselves.

When this happens in a region, company, or in other specific surroundings or social structures, we sadly sometimes see what we call suicide clusters—multiple suicides that seem to be connected to one another. If suicidal behavior is localized in both time and geographic space, often within a community or institutional setting, this may be called a *point cluster*.

Setting up a postvention system

I was asked to advise a police chief; four police colleagues in his region had recently died by suicide. He desperately wanted to stop what he called "domino suicides." We assembled a team and assisted the police psychologists in the region to analyze the deaths and set up a postvention system. They had been investing in prevention, but postvention was new to them. The psychologists and the peer support teams in the region received continued education to perform and work with findings in psychological autopsies, looking into the backgrounds of the suicide. Safeguards were put into place and at least two colleagues were helped and their lives saved because of the new prevention program in the region.

We see clusters in many different areas, such as when young people from one school or university or several colleagues within the same company die within a short period of time.

Suicides can also be connected in other ways—for example, through the internet and social media. With many closed Facebook groups, this can be difficult to detect, as not all the groups are accessible to non-members. Several social media platforms are developing algorithms and systems to detect suicidal language and behavior online.

Combined suicides, suicide pacts, and mass suicides

Sometimes multiple people die by suicide together. When this happens, we talk about combined suicides or suicide pacts. When many people die together, we talk about mass suicides.

Mass suicides have been reported throughout history—often during wars, when defeat was near and people took their fate into their own hands. Sometimes other motives were found after mass suicides, such as in religious cults and sects. In some of these cases, evidence of wounds inflicted by others was found on some of the bodies. Bearing in mind that many vulnerable people are drawn to these cults and sects, you could argue that probably not all of them actually chose to die. That is a whole new and different subject, enough to fill a separate book.

Most of us will never encounter a case of mass suicide. But we will encounter combined suicides, also called suicide pacts.

Fatima and Jaise, a peer pact

Fatima and Jaise met in the youth center they were placed in. They both came from broken families and had been abused by their parents. They became very close friends because they had so much in common. They were both suffering from mental illness and self-harming behavior. When they started to harm themselves together and the severity kept increasing, the staff at the center decided that it would be better to move one of them. It was decided that Fatima would be transferred to a different center.

A few days before the move, the two girls did not make their curfew. That had happened before, so there was no alarm raised. While staff continued to try to contact them on their cellphones, several sirens were heard driving past the center. The two girls had both died on the railway tracks.

A long postvention process and a huge investigation followed. Changes were made in the youth care system to prevent similar disasters, because this was a disaster to so many.

Mr. and Mrs. Jones

Mr. Jones had been chief of police for decades. After he retired, he planned to travel the country with his wife and their dog. They had sold their house and bought a very fancy mobile home. During one of their trips, Mrs. Jones had suddenly become very ill. She was taken to hospital and diagnosed with pancreatic cancer. There was nothing the doctors could do to cure her. Mr. and Mrs. Jones left the hospital with very strong pain medication. They drove to visit all of their favorite places in the weeks that followed.

When the emergency services were called, they found a passer-by who had discovered a horrific scene. Their dog and both Mr. and Mrs. Jones had died from intoxication and gunshot wounds. Knowing what would follow, Mr. Jones had written instructions and an explanation to his colleagues. He could not imagine a life without his wife and would not leave his dog. Despite Mr. Jones's efforts, one of the police officers working on that exact day suffered PTSD after working the Joneses' case. He had known Mr. Jones personally. Although he received treatment and is back on the force now, on that day his life was changed.

Sadly, these situations occur. Although many of us will be able to understand Mr. Jones's decision and reasoning, the impact of these cases is still massive. In this case there were no direct relatives to be informed.

Being a part of the police family, the whole first-responder community experienced the impact. It was huge.

I have seen cases where adult children suddenly lost both of their parents. Although their parents may have thought everyone would be better off this way, my experience is that this is not always the case; especially when the deaths were completely unexpected, some bereaved people have told me they felt as if the floor was pulled away from underneath them. Here they were, adults with busy lives and their own families, suddenly becoming an orphan, without any chance of saying goodbye and receiving answers to the many questions that often remained.

Murder-suicide

This is another subject to fill a whole different book, but I will have to keep it short here.

Several years ago, we lost 150 people when a German pilot crashed his commercial plane, ending his own life and taking 149 people with him. It is important to note that there was only one death by suicide in this case. All of the other lives were violently taken.

To those of us who were coordinating the response, this meant that we needed to set up suicide postvention for the loved ones left behind by the pilot. The other bereaved families received crisis intervention and bereavement support, organized in a different way.

These major cases are rare. But murder–suicide does happen in smaller settings. And it can have a tremendous impact on those it affects.

Albert, 56, crisis intervention team member

We were called to a deadly traffic incident; a car drove on to the highway in the wrong direction. It had crashed head-on into a lorry. Both drivers of the vehicles had died on impact. The lorry driver was from a foreign country. The driver in the car could be identified because he was carrying his ID.

There were four people registered at his home address and a team of two of us went out with two police officers to inform the deceased's loved ones. As we arrived at the house, the police officer rang the bell but noticed that the front door was open. He rang again, but there was no response. The police officers asked us to wait outside as they went in. As they came out, their faces were pale. They had discovered two bodies inside.

We discovered later that the mother had been staying at her parents' house with her two children to escape domestic violence. On that tragic day the father had gone to the children's school and taken his children from the playground.

A major investigation followed and we suddenly had two police scenes. And a mother we needed to inform.

This case became a major incident within our system. And, again, different approaches were needed; only the father had died by suicide. The children's lives were violently taken. A very aggressive letter to their mother was found.

The mother's family would not let the father's parents say goodbye to the children. The father's parents had not only lost their son to suicide, but they also lost their only grandchildren. Mediation was accepted and we could support both families and attend to their needs.

The children's school was supported by another team. And peer support was set up for the many first responders involved in this case.

There are a few words you may hear when murder–suicide cases occur. I will mention them here, but only for your understanding; these "labels" are not added to a case by us, only by investigators. Bereaved people may hear them too and ask you to explain what is meant. If you encounter other words unknown to you, just find the right moment to ask colleagues at the scene to explain them to you.

Undoing describes what the father did in this case. He changed the image at the scene of his crime. After he had ended his children's lives, he dressed them up and put them on their beds, their hands folded around some flowers. He had burned candles next to them. It was if he wanted to reverse part of his actions, although clearly the damage done was irreversible.

Infanticide is the term used when a child's life is taken by another person.

Intimicide describes someone taking the life of a person within an intimate relationship.

Suicide by cop

Very rarely, people provoke situations around armed officers, creating a seemingly dangerous situation. Officers are trained to respond to situations where there is an immediate threat, using firearms when necessary.

Most people who have died in these incidents were males, many of whom were suffering from mental illness. Studies have reported that they had often communicated about suicide before they died.

When an armed officer uses their firearm and life is lost, an official inquiry will follow. This has a tremendous impact on the bereaved, but also on all the officers and other first responders involved.

It is extremely important to set up a suicide postvention plan at a very early stage after the death; communication and information management are vital.

We have seen that many people who died in these incidents went into the situation carrying fake or dummy weapons. They may have looked absolutely real to the officers involved, but they were later discovered to be fake.

You can imagine the complexity of the situation the officer has to face; they are the subject of an investigation and they have their own feelings and emotions to work through.

Officers involved in cases like this one may develop what we call *moral injury*; they respond to perceived moral transgression during this extreme event and may experience a blow to their moral conscience.

Much research is currently being done into this phenomenon and I think we will hear more about it in the future.

What is important for us to know is that these cases always have a massive impact and that it is important to set up crisis intervention for the bereaved, but also for all first responders involved, especially the officers.

Many police forces will have specialists to consult.

Farid, shot by an officer

Farid had been in and out of custody and psychiatric hospitals for several years. Police officers knew him, as he had often committed crimes or had needed mental healthcare because of psychotic episodes. They knew he had been arrested with a firearm before. On a Saturday night, after the sun had set, Farid ran up to two armed police officers with what looked like a gun in his hand. The officers immediately responded and ordered Farid to drop his gun and lie down on the floor. When he didn't and kept running towards the officers, one of them pulled the trigger. Farid died. The officers immediately started CPR, but without success. The scene was taken over by investigative colleagues from a different department. Both officers were questioned and received support from a specialized team within the police force. Farid's "gun" turned out to be a plastic water gun he had painted black. Much discussion arose in the media, which complicated the situation for everyone involved; although many people felt Farid's death could have been prevented, there were no formal charges as it was ruled that the officers had acted within protocol and followed all the rules and regulations.

When famous people end their lives

We all know examples of celebrities lost to suicide. To their near and dear ones, their loss is just as devastating as any loss to suicide. However, thousands and sometimes even millions of people may be affected by the loss of a person they have probably never met, but admired, loved, and looked up to.

If media coverage is followed by an increase in suicides, occurring within a shorter period of time than would be expected, this may be what is termed a *mass cluster*.

Brendon, identifying with an idol

Brendon was a huge fan of an actor who recently died by suicide. His room was filled with props, posters, and pillows bearing the actor's picture. Brendon identified with him because the actor had openly discussed the issues he encountered after coming out and telling his family and friends that he was gay. Brendon was gay, but he was very reluctant to talk to his religious parents. He was afraid they would disapprove. His computer showed that Brendon had Googled and read all the media coverage on the actor's death. When his mother found him, he had died under very similar circumstances, as if he had copied the actor's death. In a letter that was found next to him, he apologized to his parents. The heartbreaking part of this case was to sit with his mother afterwards. As she read the letter, she sobbed. She told me she had known Brendon was gay from a very young age. Feelings of guilt and despair filled the room; she had never dared to start a discussion and had hoped that Brendon would find the right moment to open up to her. Now it was too late. A beautiful young life lost. A loving mother broken. While driving home, I had to stop and take a few deep breaths, because tears were blocking my view.

I explained the effects of (online) communication earlier. Make sure you always have a download of media guidelines at hand. You have read about the Werther effect and the Papageno effect; we can either increase or lower the risk of suicide by our communication choices.

Many people identify with their idol and favorite celebrity. Looks and behaviors are often copied, especially by young people. If the person you admire and follow dies by suicide, this may become a valid option to escape pain and sorrow for you too; you identified with them. And you may just be able to identify with them after death. This can be a very risky situation.

If I look at headlines after a celebrity suicide, I am often very disturbed by the apparent lack of knowledge of guidelines among certain media outlets. However, more and more journalists consult us and get it right, because there is also a window of opportunity. The world lost a well-known and valued person, but in covering this news we have a chance to implement media guidelines and to talk about suicide in a safe way. We can inform people and offer them help and support. We can tell them stories of hope and healing in others. We can show the devastating impact the suicide has on all of us, and we may just motivate people to help us prevent further suicides.

Suicide and (cruise)ships

Nowadays, millions of people take cruises. We have heard about several incidents of people jumping off cruise ships. Recently, a German singer/actor went missing from a cruise ship. His body was not found. We are worried that the extended news coverage may lead to copycat behavior.

I tried to find out how often suicides occur on (cruise)ships. A few hundred cases seem to have been reported.

Cruise lines are reluctant to share information, as it may affect their business. And some people told me that the reluctance in communication is intentional because they want to prevent suicide contagion, which makes sense.

Even if they don't happen very often, suicides on (cruise)ships need specialist attention.

Thousands of people are confined in one location. If a disappearance is noticed, a ship will stop immediately and a search will be started. The whole ship and the waters will be searched, and people will be informed. This puts vulnerable people (both staff and crew) at increased risk for suicide.

Cellphones and the internet often can't be used on a ship as satellite connections are extremely expensive, so it is difficult to signpost people to helplines in their own language.

With so many people of so many nationalities on a ship, responses to the incident will differ; some people will be greatly affected by what happened, but others will want to return to normality (and their vacation) as soon as possible. This can lead to tension and conflicts.

Staff will be under tremendous pressure because they have to keep working, but they will also be subject to an investigation by the international coastguard and the police.

A disappearance may be caused by accident, but it may also turn out to be a homicide or a suicide. Often a body is never found, which complicates any investigation.

Ships all have very strict safety protocols and regulations. I suggest that more specific suicide prevention and postvention training is added to ship safety preparation; this system needs to be self-manageable during the immediate aftermath.

Crisis communication needs to be done in safe ways, both on the ship and to the outside (social) media world.

With numbers of ships and passengers sharply on the rise, I hope cruise lines will use our field expertise and competency to prepare suicide safety plans and suicide postvention strategies.

Taboo within a taboo: Autoerotic fatalities

I sincerely hope that you will read this title not knowing what I am talking about. Most of you will not encounter autoerotic fatalities, as they are rare. It is very hard to find numbers and data on the subject, because it is wrapped in taboo and shame.

The impact of these incidents is massive—on those who discover the death, on those who are left behind. Autoerotic incidents also pose an incredibly complicated situation to first responders.

So, what are we talking about?

Autoerotic deaths are accidental deaths. During solitary sexual activity, death is caused unintentionally by props or objects that are used to enhance sexual stimulation.

I have encountered several cases. In these cases, the deceased died from autoerotic asphyxia, caused by strangulation. This is the most common cause of death seen in these cases.

Technically, I need to state that autoerotic fatalities are not suicides. If there is uncertainty about whether the deceased intended suicide, the verdict may be left open. But when the case is investigated and the death is viewed as an autoerotic fatality, it is officially an unintentional or accidental death or misadventure.

Although we are not talking about suicide here, it is important to address this difficult subject.

So much taboo surrounds autoerotic accidents that I have encountered situations where the bereaved pleaded with the responding police officers to report the death as a suicide.

Karl, 68, who lost his son

I did not know what to do, how to react, or what to say to all those people in my house. They were all very respectful and kind, but I felt so very embarrassed. My heart felt like it was exploding in my chest. I was sad and angry, all at once. I had found him. My son was in his bedroom. He was dressed like a woman. Parts of his body were undressed, and he was dead. He had choked himself. The doctor sat down with me and she explained what they were thinking; the police officer said that it looked like my son had been masturbating. He had blocked the airflow to his lungs, which some people do to increase a feeling of sexual pleasure. I had barely understood that my son was dead and now they were telling me this. This could not be happening. They were taking a lot of time to explain and help, but this was just too much. How was I supposed to explain this to his mother? I couldn't and I wouldn't. So I said that I thought it would be best if the police put into their records that my son had died by suicide. I got really upset and they gave me some time to get a hold of myself. After the investigation was finished, my son was taken away and most people had left. Our GP suddenly appeared. He stayed with me. And when my wife got home, he helped me talk to her. I am forever grateful that he did.

Just imagine what Karl had to go through. First, he found his dead son, in a bizarre position and strange outfit. He did not understand what he was seeing, but he realized his son had died and he needed to call the emergency services. His house had suddenly become a police scene and all those people took over his former safe zone. They all saw his beautiful, smart son in this extremely awkward situation. Karl was not allowed to touch him or change anything from the moment the first responders arrived.

He was then told that his son had probably died by accident—that most people who die this way did not intend to die.

Autoerotic asphyxiation can become an addiction; blood flow to the brain is limited, which leads to reactions in the brain that are experienced as pleasurable.

With any addiction, a higher dose of whatever one is addicted to is needed to reach the same effect, because the body adapts to survive. If people are addicted to drugs or alcohol, more drugs or alcohol are needed to satisfy the craving.

A similar effect seems to occur in autoerotic asphyxiation; at first the flow of oxygen is blocked for a short time and whatever is used to block it is released relatively quickly. But this behavior can become addictive and the length of time the oxygen is blocked will be increased. This is extremely dangerous; if a person becomes unconscious and can't release the blockage, they will die.

There is no formal training or any response protocol nor a lot of science for these cases, but most coroners and police officers will tell you that the deaths caused by autoerotic behavior most often take the lives of young men.

Often body parts will be exposed, but sometimes they are not. The asphyxiation alone may lead to the effect the deceased was intending.

If people die from hanging, an erection and/or ejaculation may occur as a physical response to the pressure and damage to the body. We know this because hanging is still used in some parts of the world where the death penalty is active.

We sometimes see cross-dressing (as in Karl's case), mirrors, or pornography at the scene of an autoerotic death. We are all professionals, as first responders, but these scenes can make us feel very uncomfortable.

This is why I have decided to add this subject to this book; although autoerotic deaths are not suicidal deaths, it is important to inform you that they exist, although they are rare.

Let me tell you about the case that motivated me to write about this.

Sarah, 15, who lost her father, and Polly, 51, who lost her husband

Sarah

Sarah was supposed to sleep over at her friend's house, where they were having a party. She did not enjoy herself and decided to go home that night. Her mom was working a late shift and she knew her dad would be home. He did not answer the phone, but he often missed Sarah's calls, so she was not worried. Sarah saw the lights on inside her house and parked her bicycle in the shed behind the house. When she walked towards the back door, she saw her dad. It was dark, so she spoke to him. He did not respond. When she got closer, she saw that he was completely undressed, and that there was a rope, tying him to the tree house. She touched him and he felt extremely cold. Sarah let out a scream, as she realized her daddy was dead. She rushed inside, as the back door was open. Sarah went into her bedroom and hid under the covers, holding her bear and not knowing what to do. Everything seemed to go blank and time seemed to stop.

Polly

Polly had worked the late shift and drove home. Her daughter was away at a friend's for the night and she was looking forward to a quiet night with her husband. She saw the lights on inside the house as she parked in front. She called for her husband as she went in to let him know she was home, but got no response. She checked several rooms and then went out through the back to see if he was working on his motorbike in the shed. Before she got that far, she found him. He was naked and there was something tied around his neck. She took her phone from her pocket. She called the emergency number and told them to come right away; her husband needed immediate help.

Sarah and Polly continued—Ralph, 28, police officer

This was a first. I had never seen anything like it. When we got the lights up at the incident scene, it looked like a scene from a bad movie, to be honest. The body of the deceased was surrounded by toys you can buy at adult stores. My colleague and I were glad the wife was inside and there were no neighboring houses with a view. The wife had been begging us all to bring him back, to help him. But he had been dead for a while when we arrived. She did not want to accept this, which happens, and I get that. We could not proceed and had to wait for colleagues from the investigation unit to come over, but they were busy, as it was a Saturday night. What on earth had this man been doing out there? It was a very strange situation. We went inside, where the doctor and paramedics were taking the wife's blood pressure. They asked us to wait a bit because they felt she was not ready for questioning. So my colleague and I went into the hallway. There were two chairs at the top of the stairs and we decided to sit down there, because there was nothing for us to do at that moment. My colleague is a very funny guy. And we often use sarcasm as a way to deal with the bad stuff we encounter. With nobody around, we looked at each other and started to wonder what the dead man outside had been doing.

You can imagine what happened. A young girl, hidden under her covers, but with her bedroom door open, scared to bits, frozen.

Sarah continued

Sarah had heard her mom come home; she had heard her screams. But she could not move. And she felt very bad as she heard her mom shout to the paramedics to help her husband. To save him. Was he still alive? Should Sarah have helped him? Could Sarah have helped him? She felt guilty and afraid. Sarah and her mom had been having daily fights these past weeks, and just this morning Sarah had told her mom she hated her.

After a while she heard two men coming towards her room. They sat down on Grandma's chairs in the hallway. She was shocked to hear what they were saying. They were talking about her dad. And one of them even started to laugh in a very strange way.

Sarah suddenly felt very sick. There was no time to get up. She started to vomit. And she could not stop. She panicked. And suddenly two men in police uniforms pulled the covers from over her.

If one person reads this book and if one situation like Sarah's is prevented, it will have been worth the effort. Sarah and her parents live in a country where suicide postvention is not available.

The people responding had no way of knowing Sarah was there. Her mom did not know she was home. And the officers responding were not sufficiently prepared for a case like this. They did not mean to, but they caused secondary damage to Sarah, following the primary damage caused by the extreme situation of finding her father.

Damage control

The next morning I got a phone call, because this situation was very upsetting in so many ways. And I traveled to Sarah and her mom to support them.

Of course, there was no way to go back in time and change the situation, but we picked up the pieces together.

A plan was made to support Sarah and her mom through those first difficult days. Later, the school social worker and the GP were involved and took over their support.

Sometimes people mess up. Sometimes first responders mess up. But we need to learn from each and every case.

Although I sincerely hope you will not encounter autoerotic accidents, inform yourself about what is important, just in case. Here are some things to consider.

Words

Choose your words carefully; words have impact. Remember what happened in Sarah's case. Use clear, neutral words, but make sure the people you are talking to understand them; "your son died in an autoerotic accident" may be correct, but you need to explain. Be honest; be specific:

We are still investigating, but we believe your son died from a lack of oxygen. Sometimes people block their airway to reduce the flow of oxygen to the brain. This leads to an altered state of consciousness, which seems to increase sexual arousal for some. We believe that something went wrong and your son was unable to release the blockage in time. Most people who die in these circumstances don't plan to die. They die by accident.

Make sure your information is correct and verified. Not all people die from autoerotic asphyxia; some people die from other causes. If a person has died from a stroke or heart failure, for example, the death may turn out to be due to natural causes after all.

Body language

Be aware of your non-verbal communication and body language, even if you feel extremely uncomfortable with the situation, know that people may be watching you. Humor and sarcasm are coping strategies to many first responders, I am aware of that. But take extra care in these specific cases to keep a professional attitude at all times. Even if the bereaved are out of sight, others may see or hear you.

The image

Discovering the dead body of a loved one is devastating. Discovering it after an autoerotic death may even be more disturbing. If the body needs to be taken away for further investigation, see if you can find the time to create another, different image for the bereaved.

This is of even more importance if the death occurred at home; we have seen people avoiding a room or a part of their house after these deaths.

After the investigation of the scene is finished and the body is prepared for transportation, we give the bereaved a chance to go back in and see a different image. The body may be on a bed or on the coroner's stretcher. The investigators on the scene will give clear instructions about what they allow; a body may be covered, but a mother may be allowed to touch her son's face, for example. The light may be dimmed, and we may set up candles or use different rituals. It is important to explain this in advance and to let the bereaved take control:

> When you are ready, you will open the door. Your son will be inside the room, on a stretcher, about this high. His body is covered from below his chest. His eyes and mouth are closed. The police have asked us not to touch him. The lights are off and we have lit a candle next to him. There is an officer in the room with him. You can take your time. We will cover your son together and take him to the car afterwards.

Involve

Don't take over what people may be able to do themselves even though you may feel sorry for them and want to help. This will give you an action perspective, but is it helpful to the bereaved? Involve people as much as possible; find ways to help them regain control in an extreme situation. Explain who is around, what they are doing, and why this is necessary. These situations are heartbreaking and difficult for us too. The bereaved may have never heard about autoerotic risky behavior. Explain that these cases occur. You may even find bereavement support agencies connecting people with lived experience.

The suicide at the International Court of Justice

This section is adapted from a blog I wrote after it happened in November 2017.

What happened?

A former Croatian general heard his sentence at the International Court of Justice in The Hague. He was convicted for war crimes, took a vial of poison from his pocket, drank it, and later died in hospital. While we agreed in media guidelines not to show and describe methods of suicides (because we know it can trigger other suicides), reality caught up with us; there was a livestream from the courtroom and the images were all over (social) media. Some articles offered added helplines; many didn't.

When situations pose challenges, we need to face them; we can't implement guidelines retrospectively. Some media articles addressed the dilemma: Should we block the images or not? But most media outlets showed the images over and over.

I get this, from a journalist's perspective. But watching the images and reading about what happened can lead to triggering behavior in people experiencing suicidal thoughts. They are often in a mental state we call "constriction"; while experiencing tremendous suffering, our worldview changes; people describe this as similar to a kind of tunnel vision; the suffering and pain take up so much energy that they become the only point of focus. And ending one's life is a method to end this pain and suffering. We know it is not a conscious decision to "choose death," as people often call it; constriction limits our ability to make conscious decisions. If people get (professional) support, it is very possible to get well again.

So here we are; images and stories all over the internet. Knowing this can be risk-enhancing. I saw journalists struggling while covering what had happened, and I received many questions from all kinds of people. What would I recommend?

What follows?

I think it is important to explain that this suicide in court was an exceptional suicide. People in constriction won't be able to differentiate between their own situation and what they see on screen, and identification can already be seen all over social media. Transparent information is key here. I won't tell you what to think, but I will offer some background information to help you find perspectives.

What has been written?

Suicidology has been a field of science and writing for more than a century now. But suicide is as old as mankind and can be found on seven occasions in the Bible and in the writings of Seneca, Socrates, Augustine, Rousseau, Hume, and many after them, including Sigmund Freud. Although suicide is no longer a crime in Western society, we still see a huge taboo and a lot of guilt and shame surrounding suicide.

I won't go in too many directions, but there are two theories that may assist us in understanding what happened in The Hague in November 2017.

Durkheim

Durkheim was a French sociologist who wrote a book called *Le Suicide* in 1897. He focused on the impact society has on individuals. The essence of what he said was that suicide occurs when there is a disturbance in the amount of control a society holds over an individual; this control becomes either too weak or too strong.

On the one hand, he saw suicide as being demanded as the utmost honorable deed to serve society (an example is Harakiri); there was no other option and this suicide was simply dictated by society

Then there is the opposite kind of suicide; when connections and bonding to society are lost, a person can experience utter hopelessness and despair. People feel disconnected, lost, and lonely. If you look at the information above, these are people who experience constriction. Most suicides we see result from this kind of disconnection to society and reality.

Durkheim came up with a third, very sudden kind of suicide; sometimes there is an extreme event causing immediate disruption between an individual and society. This can be a sudden death of a loved one, but also immediate loss of status or wealth. Nowadays, some people speak of "impulsive" suicide in this sense. This is not always the case; sometimes acute stress can lead to immediate suicidal thoughts, but we often see change when adrenaline and cortisol levels come down. This wasn't exactly what Durkheim meant; he was talking about what he named "anomie"—a sudden and total cutting of connections, like the ropes keeping a ship in port.

So there is Durkheim. And if you take on his perspective, you see something very interesting (well, at least I do). We have all seen the clip of the suspect in court. He hears his verdict. He voices his disrespect and then takes the poison. Looking at this, Durkheim would speak of total anomie; a sudden disconnection of the suspect and his surroundings. But if you have seen the images of the people at home, still supporting this former general, they characterized his death as an honorable one; to them he died as a martyr for the greater cause. It shows how complicated this is. Very importantly, Durkheim's perspective gives us an opportunity to differentiate and address identification; this suicide may be placed in the first or third category, but certainly not in the second one.

Baechler

Fast-forward to 1978, when a man called Jean Baechler wrote about suicide. He was not trained in medicine, philosophy, or sociology; he was a historian. He posed something very simple: "Suicide denotes all behavior that seeks and finds the solution to an existential problem by making an attempt on the life of the subject." He described four types of suicide:

- suicide as a way to escape a life that has become intolerable (again, most suicides we see would fall into this category)

- suicide motivated by aggression

- suicide as a kind of self-sacrifice, motivated by "higher values"

- suicide done while engaging in thrill-seeking behavior. Nowadays we might call them incidents or accidents. An example is a death during Russian roulette.

Again, back to the suicide in court. The man's supporters may see this death as self-sacrificial. But to me, with an outside perspective, I thought the way the suicide was planned and performed carried a tremendous amount of aggression; at the moment the verdict was pronounced, the suspect lost control over his future. And taking the poison was a way for him to take back control over his situation. This is what typically happens in aggression; aggression is not an emotion. It is behavior to find a way to take back control, when control is or seems lost. I read that the deceased had forbidden his loved ones to attend the court hearing. A lot of preparation went ahead. While the images made me feel this aggression, I also felt very sad in a way; by choosing this way to die, he decided to leave alone, depriving his family and loved ones of the chance to say goodbye or be with him. Just like the theory above, Baechler also makes it easy for us to differentiate and address identification here; we would not place this suicide in the first category, as we would most suicides we see.

Conclusion

So, there you have my personal insights into the background information I used to make sense of this situation myself. I don't have all the answers and suicide is of huge concern to those of us working in prevention and postvention. As with any complex subject, dialogue is very important; alone we can do so little, but together we can do so much.

My thoughts and prayers are with the bereaved in this case, but also with the witnesses and the first responders attending to this suicide. It is also with those who suffered war crimes, awaited this day of justice, and had to witness what happened just after justice was pronounced. Peace be with them, in so many ways.

CHAPTER 6—SUMMARY

- If children are bereaved, there are many ways to involve them during the aftermath of a suicide.

- When celebrities die by suicide, safe communication is of vital importance.

- Suicide clusters can be seen in different areas, when multiple people die by suicide in a short period of time or in a certain area.

- Combined suicides or mass suicides can occur if people end their lives together.

- Murder-suicide occurs when someone ends another person's life and afterwards ends their own life by suicide. These cases often happen in family settings and have a massive impact on everyone confronted with them.

- When someone dies after provoking armed officers to use their firearms, this is called suicide by cop.

- Autoerotic fatalities are *not* suicides; people die by accident when methods used to increase sexual stimulation accidentally cause death. These cases are loaded with heavy feelings of shame and are devastating to the bereaved.

- Be informed that these cases do happen. Respond professionally.

- Suicides on cruise ships don't happen very often, but when they do, they can have a huge impact. When there are thousands of people contained on a vessel without access to helplines, it is important that staff members are trained and skilled to respond.

- Sometimes media confront us with sudden images.

- In 2017 we were confronted with a suicide on live TV at the International Court of Justice.

- If this happens and images are all over the media, it is important to counter them with guidance and advice.

7

Conclusions: Moving
on After Suicide

This is a short section about the road ahead for both the bereaved
and for us as first responders.

Bereavement by suicide is a complicated kind of bereavement. There's
the sudden loss of someone near and dear to you. You were left out
of their last decisions, their last steps and actions; they went alone.
There is also the sudden confrontation with a body, the aftermath
of an investigation, potentially traumatizing circumstances, severe
reactions, and tremendous feelings of guilt and shame. These are just a
few examples of factors that may cause grieving to be very complicated.

If you look into the literature on grief, you will find several models
and timelines of how grief is supposed to develop. Don't try to look for
a fixed protocol on grief after suicide. You won't find it. People need
time, space, and, often, support to sail these extremely stormy waters
after suicide.

Be a lighthouse to them, when direction seems to be lost.

Louis, 36, who lost his twin brother to suicide

I had lost loved ones before, but when I lost my twin brother to suicide it
felt like the volume on my grief was turned up over the maximum I could
handle. I felt like I was thrown on to a rollercoaster and I couldn't get off
it. Just when I thought the rollercoaster had reached a straight track, it
would suddenly go into a loop again. It took me a while to find my way

out of it. But I will never be the same again. There is my life before the suicide, and there is my life after his suicide. A part of me is missing, and my world will never be as beautiful as it was.

As you have read in this book, those bereaved by suicide are at an increased risk of suicide themselves, or they may experience other severe complications.

But it is very important to share with you that most of them will find ways to cope and move on. As Louis described, many bereaved people will speak about life before and life after the suicide. Their world has changed forever. But at some point, they find ways to cope and function again.

More and more people have joined us in fighting for better understanding and support for those confronted with and bereaved by suicide. Many of them are bereaved by suicide themselves. In working with them and looking at them, I see what people mean when they talk about *post-traumatic growth*.

This book is about the immediate phase after a suicide. It is far too early to talk about this phenomenon then. But it is important for me to show you how powerful it can be when people bereaved by suicide share help and hope.

Dr. Sharon McDonnell lost her brother to suicide. She became a suicidology researcher and developed evidence-based training on suicide postvention. Sharon is currently leading the largest study ever done into suicide postvention. Her findings will be presented to policy makers and show us what people bereaved by suicide really need. Every year, Sharon brings together more than 400 delegates from many countries to learn and share about suicide bereavement. I am honored to be a member of her Suicide Bereavement UK team. You will find a link to our work in the Resources list.

Angela Samata lost her life partner to suicide. She was left behind as a young mother and had many questions and worries. Her search for answers to some of them was filmed by the BBC. Angela's documentary received a BAFTA nomination and was viewed by millions. Angela is inspiring many of us by leading the way in suicide prevention. She has co-produced a free online course to train people on how to support suicidal people. Links to both the documentary and the course are in the Resources list. I can highly recommend them!

Psycho-hygiene: What about us?

Working after suicide is demanding; you never get used to it and it will never get easy. If it does feel that way, you may need some serious supervision. A suicide is a major critical incident to those confronted with it. Every suicide has a huge impact on all of us.

As first responders, we have to attend many different cases, suicide among them. And we are not just first responders; we have different roles and responsibilities besides our jobs.

A few years ago my daughter was diagnosed with a tumor in the head. I wanted to continue working, but I also had to deal with a lot of uncertainty and concern. I decided to not take on first-response calls during those months and just took on planned work such as training. After my daughter had recovered from surgery, I went back to my normal schedule.

Whenever you fly, you get the same drill: If pressure is lost in the cabin, oxygen masks will drop down. Please put on your own oxygen mask first before you go and help others.

The same applies to us: Take care of yourself. You can't and shouldn't go out to help others when you are in a vulnerable state yourself; it is OK to not be OK. Well meant is not always well done.

And setting personal boundaries is a sign of professionalism, not of weakness. Use your team intervision meetings and your personal supervision moments to reflect. Peer support is so very important; be there for each other and know that others are also available for you.

As responders confronted with suicide, we are at an increased risk of suicide ourselves. As you will learn in suicide prevention training, reach out when you are concerned: see, say, and signpost.

A few things to watch when taking care of yourself:

- Respect confidentiality.

- Remember you are working with vulnerable people; extreme reactions and emotions are not personal. Be safe and stay safe.

- Don't confuse sympathy with empathy; always keep a professional distance.

- If you feel a case causes too much identification or just comes too close, don't be afraid to talk about this. When possible, refer it to a colleague.

- Set time limits and plan the number of hours you work, and factor in recovery time.

- Delegate and refer when needed; you don't have to do everything yourself and on your own.

- Take breaks and vacations.

- Always work with others; implement team intervision, and make sure you have personal supervision.

- Make sure you get enough sleep.

- Limit your use of alcohol and/or drugs.

- Move, exercise, and help your body to work off stress hormones.

- Eat healthy meals, spreading them throughout the day, and drink plenty of water.

- Accept that you can't change a situation; being there, your ministry of presence, may be all you can offer.

To the world you are just one person, but to one person you could mean the world.

As this book comes to an end, I want to thank you for taking the time to read about some very difficult subjects. Know that you are doing an incredibly important job when supporting people bereaved by suicide.

I am grateful for the trust and confidence I have received from people when they allowed me into their lives on a very dark day. We only met for a short time, and I had to leave them as they had to start the long journey through grief. I hope and pray they were able to find healing and hope.

This poem is for all of them:

Spring and Grief

I see my Love in every little child
Whose eyes meet mine with laughter in their blue;
I hear him in the note, half sweet, half wild,
When bird calls bird their promise to renew;
I feel him in the ardor of the sun
That woos the fragrance from the waking flower,
And maple buds, rose flushed by beauty, won

To swift fulfilment of the Sun God's power.
The world is young once more as he was young,
With life and love reborn in everything—
O singing hearts! My own is faint and wrung;
The rapture and the riot of the Spring
Can but enhance the throb of my despair—
I miss him most when joy is everywhere!

Corinne Roosevelt Robinson (1861–1933)

I will leave you with a second poem. Remembering all those who were lost. I never met them but got to know them through their loved ones' tears and laughter. I wish I could tell them how much they are loved and missed by those who were left behind.

Remember

Remember me when I am gone away,
Gone far away into the silent land;
When you can no more hold me by the hand,
Nor I half turn to go yet turning stay.
Remember me when no more day by day
You tell me of our future that you planned:
Only remember me; you understand
It will be late to counsel then or pray.
Yet if you should forget me for a while
And afterwards remember, do not grieve:
For if the darkness and corruption leave
A vestige of the thoughts that I once had,
Better by far you should forget and smile
Than that you should remember and be sad.

Christina Rossetti (1830–1894)

CONCLUSIONS—SUMMARY

- Suicide bereavement is a very complicated kind of bereavement.
- There is no fixed timeline or protocol for grief after suicide.
- People's lives will be changed forever.

- Most people will eventually find ways to cope without professional help.

- Sometimes people even use their lived experience to help others.

- Working after suicide is very demanding to you, as a responder.

- Peer support, team intervision, and supervision are important.

- Implement psycho-hygiene.

- Don't just take care of others; take good care of yourself too.

Resources

For reference and further reading (all online downloads are free)
International helplines
International Association for Suicide Prevention (IASP)—www.iasp. info/resources/Crisis_Centres

Suicide Bereavement UK
Information on our research, conferences, and training—https:// suicidebereavementuk.com

For crisis support after suicide—https://suicidebereavementuk.com/ corporate-crisis-consultation-after-suicide

WHO publications
On suicide prevention and data—www.who.int/mental_health/suicide-prevention/en

On suicide myths—www.who.int/mental_health/suicide-prevention/ myths.pdf

On communication (two downloads, one for quick reference, one for further reading, with links to science at the back)—www.who.int/ mental_health/suicide-prevention/resource_booklet_2017/en

Article on the "holiday suicide myth"
https://cdn.annenbergpublicpolicycenter.org/Downloads/Releases/ ACI/Holiday%20Suicide%20release%202010.pdf

UK information on coroner services
www.gov.uk/government/publications/guide-to-coroner-services-and-coroner-investigations-a-short-guide

Inquest handbook—www.inquest.org.uk/useful-resources

AAS (American Association of Suicidology) statement on the difference between suicide and physician-assisted dying/euthanasia
https://suicidology.org/wp-content/uploads/2019/07/AAS-PAD-Statement-Approved-10.30.17-ed-10-30-17.pdf

How many people are exposed to suicide?
https://onlinelibrary.wiley.com/doi/full/10.1111/sltb.12450

https://www.sciencemag.org/news/2019/08/geography-loss-global-look-uneven-toll-suicide

Link to the hub where support organizations in the UK work together
http://supportaftersuicide.org.uk

Link to UK self-help groups
www.uk-sobs.org.uk

Booklet for people bereaved by suicide
Order printed copies by quoting 2901502/Help is at hand at www.orderline.dh.gov.uk

Or download at http://supportaftersuicide.org.uk/support-guides/help-is-at-hand

Download booklet for people supporting those bereaved by suicide
http://judimeadows.com/wp-content/uploads/Finding-the-words-online-version.pdf

Online suicide prevention training (see, say, signpost)
www.relias.co.uk/zero-suicide-alliance/form

Online psychological first-aid training
www.coursera.org/learn/psychological-first-aid

On stress
http://selyeinstitute.org/wp-content/uploads/2013/06/The-legacy-of-Hans-Selye44.pdf

Life After Suicide, BBC documentary by Angela Samata
https://documentaryheaven.com/life-after-suicide

Brené Brown on the difference between guilt and shame
www.youtube.com/watch?v=DqGFrId-IQg

Brené Brown on the difference between empathy and sympathy
www.youtube.com/watch?v=1Evwgu369Jw

Short video on suicide prevention
www.youtube.com/watch?v=rCa8CmqcBOc

Recommended books
To read with children
Beyond the Rough Rock: Supporting a Child Who Has Been Bereaved through Suicide by Di Stubbs and Julie Stokes (Cheltenham, UK: Winston's Wish, ISBN 9780953912377)

Everywhere and All Around by Pimm van Hest (New York: Clavis Publishing, ISBN 9781605372693)

Samantha Jane's Missing Smile: A Story about Coping with the Loss of a Parent by Julie Kaplow and Donna Pincus (Washington, DC: Magination Press, ISBN 9781591478089)

On trauma
The Body Keeps the Score: Mind, Brain and Body in the Transformation of Trauma by Bessel van der Kolk (New York: Penguin, ISBN 9780141978611)

Post-Traumatic Stress by Stephen Regel and Stephen Joseph (Oxford: Oxford University Press, ISBN 9780198758112)

On suicide and suicidology

The work of Edwin Shneidman is highly recommended. The following downloadable article will give you an overview of his work and publications: www.suicidology-online.com/pdf/SOL-2010-1-5-18.pdf

After the Suicide: Helping the Bereaved to Find a Path from Grief to Recovery by Kari Dyregrov, Einar Plyhn, and Gudrun Dieserud (London: Jessica Kingsley Publishers, ISBN 9781849052115)

Comprehending Suicide: Landmarks in 20th-Century Suicidology by Edwin S. Shneidman (Washington, DC: American Psychological Association, ISBN 1557987432)

The Suicidal Mind by Edwin S. Shneidman (New York: Oxford University Press, ISBN 0195103661)

On crisis intervention

Crisis Intervention Handbook, 3rd Edition, by Albert R. Roberts (New York: Oxford University Press, ISBN 9780195179910)

Crisis Intervention Strategies by Richard K. James (Belmont, CA: Thomson, ISBN 9781111186784)

On pastoral emergency support

Crisis Counseling: A Guide for Pastors and Professionals by Scott Floyd (Grand Rapids, MI: Kregel Publications, ISBN 9780825425882)

For German readers

Warum hast du uns das angetan? Ein Begleitbuch für Trauernde, wenn sich jemand das Leben genommen hat by Chris Paul (München: Wilhelm Goldmann, ISBN 9783442173259)

Papa hat sich erschossen by Saskia Jungnikl (Frankfurt am Main: S. Fischer, ISBN 9783596030729)

Wenn die Not Worte verschlingt by Jutta Unruh, Claudia Geese, Frank Müllenmeister, Harald Karutz, Joachim Müller-Lange, and Uwe Rieske (Pfalzfeld: Kontrast, ISBN 9783941200326)

Link to the PSNV (Psychosoziale Notfallversorgung) German government website—www.bbk.bund.de/DE/AufgabenundAusstattung/Krisenmanagement/PsychKM/Qualitaetssicherung/Qualitaet ssicherung_PSNV_einstieg.html